Du Pont

THE
DU PONTS

HOUSES AND GARDENS

IN THE BRANDYWINE

1900–1951

THE DU PONTS

HOUSES AND GARDENS IN THE BRANDYWINE

1900–1951

MAGGIE LIDZ

ESTATE HISTORIAN

WINTERTHUR MUSEUM & COUNTRY ESTATE

FOREWORD BY
GEORGE A. WEYMOUTH

ACANTHUS PRESS

NEW YORK : 2009

ACANTHUS PRESS, LLC
1133 BROADWAY, ROOM 1229
NEW YORK, NEW YORK 10010
WWW.ACANTHUSPRESS.COM
212-414-0108

COPYRIGHT © 2009, THE HENRY FRANCIS DU PONT WINTERTHUR MUSEUM, INC.

Every reasonable attempt has been made to identify the owners of copyright. Errors of omission will be corrected in subsequent printings of this work.

All rights reserved. This book may not be reproduced in whole or in any part (except by reviewers for the public press) without written permission from the publisher.

Library of Congress Cataloging-in-Publication Data

Lidz, Maggie, 1958-
  The Du Ponts, Houses and Gardens in the Brandywine, 1900-1951 / Maggie Lidz
    p. cm.
  Includes bibliographical references and index.
  ISBN 978-0-926494-69-5 (hardcover)
 1. Architecture, Domestic--Brandywine Creek Valley (Pa. and Del.) 2. Architecture--Brandywine Creek Valley (Pa. and Del.)--History--20th century. 3. Gardens--Brandywine Creek Valley (Pa. and Del.) 4. Du Pont family--Homes and haunts--Brandywine Creek Valley (Pa. and Del.) I. Henry Francis du Pont Winterthur Museum. II. Title.

NA7235.D32L53 2009
728.09751--dc22
                    2009011721

FRONTISPIECE: THE WINTERTHUR ESTATE, CA. 1920, WATERCOLOR BY A. ENOULT

PRINTED IN CHINA

CONTENTS

Acknowledgments 7

Foreword 9

Introduction 13

ELEUTHERIAN MILLS
Residence of Eleuthère Irénée du Pont
28

LOWER LOUVIERS
Residence of William Winder Laird Jr.
38

OLD NEMOURS
Residence of Eugene du Pont
44

PELLEPORT
Residence of Louisa Gerhard du Pont and Evelina du Pont
52

SAINT AMOUR
Residence of Mary Belin du Pont
58

808 BROOM STREET & THE OLD MILL
Residence of T. Coleman du Pont
69

LONGWOOD
Residence of Pierre Samuel du Pont
75

NEMOURS
Residence of Alfred I. duPont
84

GIBRALTAR
Residence of H. Rodney and Isabella du Pont Sharp
92

OWL'S NEST
Residence of Eugene du Pont Jr.
100

SECOND OFFICE
Residence of E. Paul du Pont
107

GRANOGUE
Residence of Irénée du Pont
112

CHEVANNES
Residence of Bessie G. du Pont
118

BOXWOOD
Residence of George P. and Natalie du Pont Edmonds
123

WINTERTHUR
Residence of Henry Francis du Pont
129

GARDEN CLUB OF AMERICA TOUR
Rare Images of du Pont Gardens
140

APPLECROSS
Residence of Donald and Wilhelmina du Pont Ross
148

MEOWN FARM
Residence of Isabella du Pont Sharp
154

FAIR HILL
Residence of E. Frances du Pont Morgan Rust
158

BELLEVUE
Residence of William du Pont Jr.
166

HOD HOUSE
Residence of Crawford and Margaretta du Pont Greenewalt
170

MT. CUBA
Residence of Lammot du Pont and Pamela Copeland
175

OBEROD
Residence of Harry and Jane du Pont Lunger
182

TULIP HOLLOW
Residence of Samuel Eldon and Victorine du Pont Homsey
187

THE COTTAGE AT WINTERTHUR
Residence of Henry Francis du Pont
194

Portfolio of Houses 202

Endnotes 212

Bibliography 219

Index 221

Illustration Credits 227

ACKNOWLEDGMENTS

This book is dedicated to Hazle Edens, her mother, and grandmother,
as well as Karen Farquhar, her mother, and grandmother.

I began this project ten years ago while working with the inestimable architectural historian Damie Stillman. I was fortunate to have him as an adviser for my master's thesis at the University of Delaware. Professor Stillman and Winterthur's wonderful librarian Neville Thompson encouraged my first efforts in this direction. I thank them. The late John A. H. Sweeney also helped open the first doors for this project, and I miss him every day.

Each page of the publication is a collaboration with editor Onie Rollins, and I am grateful for all her help. Winterthur's archivist Heather Clewell and librarian Helena Richardson were active participants as well, and I thank them for their time and effort. My colleagues at Winterthur—J. Thomas Savage, Jeff Groff, Robert Davis, and Chris Strand—have not only shared their great knowledge but also afforded me the time to undertake the extensive research and writing.

Of course, I would not have been able to write this book without the assistance of the du Pont family. In particular I thank the following for generously sharing their memories and photographs: Joan Bolling, the late Bruce Bredin, Ann Brown, Carroll Carpenter, Mary Kaye Phelps Carpenter, Robert Ruliph Morgan Carpenter III, Nancy Cooch, Everitt du Pont, Henry Belin du Pont IV, Irénée du Pont, Richard S. du Pont, William H. du Pont, Hazle Edens, Andrew Edmonds Jr., Leatrice Elliman, Karen Farquhar, Nancy Frederick, Katharine Gahagan, Marilyn and Nathan Hayward, Martina and Pierre Hayward, Samuel Hobbs, Don Homsey, Ann Horsey, Henry Ridgely Horsey, Irene Jennings, Brett Jones, Ethel Kinsalla, Marion Lassen, Julia B. Leisenring, Nicole Limbocher, Ruth Lord, David Lunger, Irénée May, Katherine Maroney, Lisa Moseley, Daphne Reese, Ann von Rosenstiel, Sheila Ross, Donnan Sharp, Elizabeth and William Sharp, Hugh Rodney Sharp III, Mary Laird Silvia, Margaretta Stabler, Wendie Stabler, George A. Weymouth, Ann Wick, and Phyllis Wyeth.

This history leans heavily on the du Pont family manuscript collection at Hagley Museum, one of the best, if not *the* best, family collections in the country. Dan Muir generously supplied the mounted photos from his du Pont family houses exhibition, which proved to be an invaluable resource. The foundation for much of the manuscript was provided by the excellent work of Hagley's former curators Maureen Quimby and Philip G. Correll and current curator Debra Hughes. Many of the photographs come from Hagley, and without the support and hard work of Ben Blake, Tanya Brun, Marge McNinch, Max Moeller, Terry Snyder, Judy Stevenson, and Jon Williams, this project would not have been completed.

Everyone at the du Pont–related institutions has been fantastically generous. I thank Sandy Reber and Colvin Randall at Longwood; Grace Gary and Francesca Bonny at Nemours; Susan Matsen Maynard, formerly of Nemours; Denise

ACKNOWLEDGMENTS

Magnani, Cara Lee Blume, Dorothy Payton, and Judy Jeffers at Bellevue; Rick Lewandowski and Ann Holloway at Mt. Cuba; Nedda Moqtaderi and Jody Cross for the work they did on Mt. Cuba; Connie Walsh, Janet Sheridan, Anne Verplanck, Lin and Henry White, Leslie Bottero, and particularly Melinda Penn at Greenville Country Club (the former Owl's Nest).

Many of the houses described here are still in private hands, and I received invaluable help and cooperation from Dr. and Mrs. William Norwood, Steven and Lisa Frankel, William Prickett, Jill Cantera, Rob Moore, Linda Hall, Virginia Brawders, Vance Kershner, Ronald Finch, Laura Canter, Tracy Willman, Mary Malony, Cynthia Farris, Bill Gotwals, Joseph Carbonell, and Carey Hedlund.

I would also like to give special thanks to Lonnie Dobbs, Robert Raley, Barksdale Maynard, Patt Cannon, and Richard Dayton for the knowledge they shared with me. Thanks to Barry Cenower for giving me the opportunity to write this book and for all his support; and to Dalia Stoniene at Acanthus Press for her hard work. Last but not least, thanks most of all to my patient husband, Franz Lidz.

FOREWORD

IT WAS A SPLENDID day for a turn around Rencourt: dark, damp, forbidding. Beneath the towering trees that seemed, to my nine-year-old eyes, to bathe this Edwardian mansion in perpetual gloom, my sister Patty and I snuck into the place we thought was a ghost house. Built by my great-grandfather Alexis Irénée du Pont in 1890 for his wife, Elizabeth Canby Bradford, Rencourt was permanently shuttered after her death in 1925. For Patty and me—20 years on—the granite house was a spooky playground. We drifted in a sea of gargoyles and Tiffany glass and dusty Victorian furniture. I helped Patty squeeze into the laundry chute and listened with glee as she screamed all the way down. Then she slid down the banister of the staircase that was so wide you could have driven a Jeep up the steps.

To a child, Rencourt was the most enchanting of the great du Pont houses, none of which were exactly architectural wonders. I grew up in Doggone, the house my grandparents gave my mother and father as a wedding gift in 1930. Much of my youth was misspent across the field at Dogwood, my grandparents' house. My grandmother Catherine Dulcinea Moxham was from Louisville, and my grandfather Eugene E. du Pont had built her a Kentucky mansion. She was afraid of fire, which is why Dogwood was constructed with concrete—the exterior clapboards, the rose trellis, everything. My grandmother loved stone, and boulders were everywhere: inside the house as columns, outside, lining the drive. She may have thought she was the White Rock Girl. The house had enormous concrete columns, and when my mother toured the Acropolis in Athens she was terribly disappointed. "The columns at Dogwood are much larger!" I always had fun in that house; the flat, red roof doubled as a skating rink. We used to stay overnight at Christmas, and my most vivid memory of Dogwood was the bedroom ceiling, which was dominated by a painting of a grinning cowboy. The hall fireplace was large enough that even with the fire blazing, Billy Driscoll, my grandfather's chauffeur, could shimmy down the chimney dressed as Santa. I loved that house almost as much as my grandfather hated horses. He once observed, "The front end bites, the back end stinks, and the middle's damned uncomfortable."

Doggone still stands, but Rencourt was demolished in the 1950s, and Dogwood was knocked down a decade later. When Dogwood met the wrecking ball, I remember thinking, "How, tragic!"

For the last four decades I have lived in an old stone house on the Brandywine River, part of which was built in 1640 by Swedish traders. The second and third floor, as well as the attic, were added in 1750 by Captain Harry Gordon, an English engineer. By the 1920s, however, the house was abandoned and in grave disrepair. It's been carefully restored and is nestled in an oxbow bend on the Brandywine. Hence the name The Big Bend, or Quineomissinque, which is what the Lenape Indians called it when it was their village.

I feel a kinship with my ancestors whose lives and interests were ruled by the land. In the mid-1960s, when I learned that the beauty of the Brandywine might be permanently disrupted by the construction of a hardhat factory in Chadds Ford, I teamed up with some friends to buy 40 acres of riparian meadowland. The Brandywine Conservancy was

FOREWORD

George A. Weymouth, portrait of Eugene E. du Pont, 1958

FOREWORD

born. We had to raise $300,000, which was a lot of money at a time when nobody talked about the environment and conservation. Ecology was a whole new dirty word. Today, the Conservancy protects 40,000 acres of open space in Delaware and Pennsylvania, mostly through conservation easements. These acres include the King Ranch near Unionville, many acres along the flood plains of the Brandywine River, portions of the Brandywine battlefield, as well as all of Winterthur.

Many books have been written about the du Ponts, from many different perspectives. Quite a few center on individual houses: Mt. Cuba, Longwood, Winterthur, Eleutherian Mills. Though several family places have become well known as museums, there are still numerous houses and gardens whose history and design tell a much larger and particularly American story. With so many destroyed, Maggie Lidz's book not only documents my family's varied architectural contribution to the Brandywine River Valley but also reveals how that contribution expresses our industrial, economic, and personal history. Her book adds considerably to our greater understanding of the 20th century.

—— George A. Weymouth

"Dogwood," Eugene E. du Pont residence, photo ca. 1950

Brandywine Valley du Pont estates of 40 acres or more, 1920–40

INTRODUCTION

NO AMERICAN FAMILY has dominated the industrial and residential architecture of a state longer than the du Ponts of Delaware. Since the 1930s, the region in which the du Ponts have settled has been called Chateau Country, a term that rankles the family, which justly prides itself on its relative simplicity and record of philanthropy. To outsiders the phrase keys into at least three characteristics that distinguish this particular place. First, the French word *chateau* conjures up the heritage apparent in the family, the houses, and the old railroad-stop names. However inaccurate a stylistic or architectural description, the phrase also suggests the du Ponts' outsize houses and properties. Finally, the term Chateau Country brings to mind a grouping of estates that, until after World War II, fit together as neatly as a jigsaw puzzle.

The du Pont family presence on Delaware soil dates to 1802, when Eleuthère Irénée du Pont settled on the banks of the Brandywine Creek and established a gunpowder mill. Unlike many other successful industrial American families, the du Ponts stayed close to the original source of their wealth. Mrs. Lammot du Pont Copeland recalled in 1935 that "if had it not been that Mr. H. B. du Pont had just about completed building his house right next door to us, I don't think that Mr. Copeland would have ever left the Brandywine." The distance between her home of Mt. Cuba and the Brandywine Creek is less than four miles.[1]

E. I. du Pont originally selected the remote rural location outside Wilmington to minimize the impact of possible industrial accidents. The du Ponts were so isolated that until the Civil War, the primary language used among family members was French, although it had developed into a kind of patois, Brandywine French they called it. The du Ponts—engineers, chemists, and administrators—worked and lived alongside their employees. They shared equally in the ever-present danger of explosives manufacturing. No one was completely safe. E. I. du Pont's father and wife never recovered from injuries suffered in accidental blasts. His youngest son and his most talented grandnephew died in separate blasts. The family's dwellings, called partnership houses, were close to the mill and, like the workers' houses, sustained continual damage. To reduce individual loss, the family practiced communal property sharing. Throughout the 19th century, horses, carriages, land, and houses were all held by the company and allotted as necessary. E. I. du Pont's son Henry, known as Boss Henry, took over in 1850 and strictly enforced the tradition of communalism, which did have a number of advantages. The family farm was able to feed multiple households; extra horses were available on request; and the close household groupings fostered a strong feeling of community. It was, however, also a situation that discouraged pride of ownership. Boss Henry's grandnephew Pierre Samuel du Pont, who later became president of the company, said of his childhood in a partnership house: "I do not remember any repapering, inside repainting, new window hangings, or new carpeting."[2]

P. S. du Pont grew up during the company's early boom years. The lack of interior decoration in his parents' home belied the fact that his father and the rest of the family were growing rich. By the end of the Civil War, the company controlled 42 percent of the national gunpowder market. Within 30 years, it was operating 28 of the 32 gunpowder mills in the

INTRODUCTION

Baroness Hyde de Neuville, drawing of Eleutherian Mills and mill buildings, ca. 1817

country. Outsiders appraised the combined family fortune at upwards of $100 million.[3]

With wealth and time, family lore and traditions emerged. During the 19th century, many Americans looked to Europe for a sense of history, and the du Ponts were no exception. As the family became Americanized, relics of their French heritage took on increasing importance. "New Year's Day Calling" was carefully observed by the du Ponts, who credited it to their French patrimony. Ancestral portrait miniatures were copied and scaled into full-size paintings, and at least three marble reproductions were made of a pair of plaster portrait busts of E. I. du Pont's grandparents. The names Pierre, Irénée, Eleuthera, and Victorine were passed down as dutifully as heirlooms. Architecturally, there was a distinct preference for French-style casement windows, tiled roofs, and stuccoed walls.

In 1846 Eleuthera du Pont Smith, the first of E. I. du Pont's children born in the United States, made a pilgrimage to Bois-des-Fossés, the country house in France where her grandparents, parents, and elder siblings had lived before coming to America. Located about 60 miles south of Paris, Bois-des-Fossés was acquired by E. I.'s father, Pierre Samuel, in 1774–75 and sold in 1808 after the family left. Smith was the first of many du Ponts to visit the house. By the turn of the 20th century, Bois-des-Fossés was an almost mandatory stop on du Pont European grand tours.[4] An Old World ancestral home gave patina to the new money rolling in from the gunpowder mills.

The du Pont family travels had almost an immediate effect on the landscape of Delaware. In the 1880s, Colonel Henry Algernon du Pont, president of the Wilmington & Northern Railroad, renamed many of the station stops after the French pedigree: Cossart, Guyencourt, Montchanin. About the same time, the family made a more regular practice of naming their houses after 18th-century French family connections: Pelleport, Rencourt, and Nemours. In the past, the du Ponts had appropriated names from earlier communities (Hagley, Rokeby) or personal associations (Eleutherian Mills). House names tended to be fluid in the 19th century. Two were called

Tourism at Bois-des-Fossés, France, 1929

Hagley. Around midcentury, Eleutherian Mills morphed into Nemours and then reverted back at the turn of the 20th century. It is unclear when the nearby 1824 house, positioned next door to Eleutherian Mills, became the current Nemours. In the late 1800s, social forms regarding house names varied, suggesting a new custom. On April 3, 1889, Elsie du Pont wrote to her cousin Pauline (Mary Pauline Foster du Pont), "I do not know whether you like your letters addressed Winterthur or not. Aunt Meta prefers to have Goodstay on hers, Aunt Mary does not like Rokeby, and I am in doubt about you."[5]

The size of the du Pont houses grew in relation to their wealth and worldliness. In the early 1870s, Swamp House (a name originally conferred in jest) was enlarged to 13 bedrooms.[6] An addition was built onto Hagley in 1879, with another constructed in 1889. A fourth floor was added to Winterthur in 1884. A group of new houses (Vireaux, 1877; Pelleport, 1881; Rencourt, 1890; Saint Amour, 1892) was built west of the Brandywine on Kennett Pike, a well-traveled thoroughfare connecting Delaware to Pennsylvania. Rencourt, Pelleport, and Vireaux were designed by architect Theophilus Parsons Chandler, a founder of the University of Pennsylvania School of Architecture and husband of Sophie du Pont, Boss Henry's youngest daughter. The first floor of Rencourt, a 3½-story stone mansion, covered nearly 3,000 square feet. Another 3½-story structure, the Albert Dilks–designed Saint Amour, had a thousand more feet of space on its first floor. According to legend, when Colonel Henry Algernon du Pont expanded Winterthur in 1902, he insisted that his architects measure the rest of the family homes to ensure his would be the largest. By 1904 the first floor of Winterthur was 4,900 square feet.

When family members gathered at Saint Amour on January 1, 1900, to celebrate their first 100 years in America, 14 family houses were located within a three-mile radius: Eleutherian Mills, Upper Louviers, Lower Louviers, Nemours, Hagley, Hagley House, Winterthur, Rencourt, Pelleport, Rokeby, Swamp Hall, Saint Amour, Goodstay, and Vireaux. Eight were partnership houses owned by the company, but the communal

INTRODUCTION

DuPont mill buildings with Eleutherian Mills in the background, ca. 1900

system, which had survived for a remarkable three generations, was giving way to private ownership. The partnership houses were old, decrepit, and undesirably close to the noisy and dangerous mills. In 1902 the company was bought out by three du Pont cousins: Alfred I., T. Coleman, and Pierre Samuel. They reshaped the 19th-century enterprise into one of most successful international corporations of the 20th century partly by selling off the extraneous residential and agricultural real estate. As they trimmed company holdings, the cousins invested privately in real estate, some of it former company land. In 1905 Alfred bought Upper Louviers and his lifelong home, Swamp Hall. The next year Pierre acquired a Pennsylvania Quaker farm in order to rescue a historic arboretum (which became Longwood), while Coleman purchased a large tract about two miles west of the Brandywine where he could farm and his wife could garden. By 1909 Alfred had acquired 400 acres of former company land for his new country estate, Nemours. These three places were the first built by the family in the new century and a harbinger of things to come.[7]

In August 1914, war orders for explosives made the du Ponts one of richest families in the world.[8] The following year, the partnership of the three cousins shattered when Coleman decided to sell his shares and enter politics. After Alfred rejected Coleman's initial offer, Pierre personally bought the shares. A bitter lawsuit pitted Alfred against Pierre. In the end, Alfred won the suit but lost the company. Pierre, by shareholders' vote—and shareholders were still mainly family members—kept control of the business.

Alfred and Pierre were as radically different as their houses. Alfred's Carrère & Hastings mansion, Nemours, was a Gilded Age whirligig of limestone, marble, bronze, glass, and gilt, equipped with every modern convenience. The decorator Charles of London arranged the ever-expanding collection of European antiques. Enclosed by a great wall, the estate had magnificent gardens and sumptuous rooms that only a select few were invited to see. In contrast, Pierre doubled the size of a modest red-brick, early 19th-century Quaker farmhouse property he called Longwood. The rooms were of modest size,

INTRODUCTION

H. F. du Pont (center) visiting his cousin Pierre (far right) at Longwood, ca. 1925

furnished with a personal muddle of American antiques and Victorian keepsakes. Pierre loved visitors and invested in spectacular fountain gardens that the public could tour every Sunday for free. His annual garden party became a du Pont family tradition. A hundred years on, nothing in the surrounding area approaches the extravagance of Alfred's Nemours, while the muted style and generous hospitality of Pierre's house at Longwood set a family standard that continues to inspire his relations today.[9]

In the 1940s Pierre asked his secretary, Margaret Kane, to research the family history and houses. His interest was due in part to a change in times and taste. In 1921 the last mill on the original Brandywine site shut down, and its houses and properties were sold. Du Pont family members were given first option and they snapped them up, remodeling the residences into stylish homes for the younger generation.[10] Late 19th-century additions and decorations were stripped away to emphasize the earliest facades. These houses, particularly Lower Louviers and Eleutherian Mills, eventually replaced Bois-des-Fossés as the locus of family history. The shift fit into the post–World War I zeitgeist that deemphasized Europe. Hollywood films and the art exhibited in the American Wing at the Metropolitan Museum of Art in New York City helped engender a new pride in American culture. The enduring success of Pierre, one of the most powerful businessmen in the country and acknowledged family patriarch, had a lot to do with his knack for adapting to change. Pierre's house at Longwood embraces a regional aesthetic that continues into the 21st century.

Pierre's brother Lammot, president of the company from 1926 to 1940, was even more low-key. Lammot raised his 10 children at Saint Amour, the rambling—but by the 1920s, distinctly unfashionable—Victorian house built by his mother. He was thrifty and unassuming, even riding his bicycle to work. During his presidency, the company controlled General Motors and U.S. Rubber and began to manufacture such synthetics as plastics, rayon, neoprene, and nylon. No matter how much money they were making, it behooved

INTRODUCTION

Workers' housing at Longwood, 1927

DuPont Company employees not to overshadow their boss, or their boss's boss, Pierre, the chairman of the board. Flamboyance was taboo.

One acceptable expression of wealth was a country house. As the company grew more successful, the landscape around Wilmington changed. Small rural farms were swallowed up into estates of various sizes, identified by enclosing walls, gatehouses, and large tracts of woodlands and fields. The 1937 *Who's Who of Commerce and Industry* included seven family members, all of whom lived within 10 miles of one another. It was at this time that the term "Chateau Country" was coined. The phrase helped explain the clannish aspect of the family. *The New York Times* noted in 1934: "The du Ponts have always had a homing instinct which leads most of them to live within easy reach of Wilmington . . . [the family hold on Delaware] has often been described as feudal."[11]

Winterthur, Nemours, Longwood, Granogue, Dripping Spigots, Owl's Nest, Bellevue, and Dilwyne Farms spanned thousands of acres and employed hundreds. Many employees stayed on for generations, their children and even grandchildren becoming estate workers. This gave the area a settled feel, perhaps accounting for the feudal attribution. Actually, 20th-century Delaware was a model of modern business practice that abided by the company commitment to scientific management, systemization of process, and the stated 1906 goals of "efficiency, economy, and permanency." It was a practical approach, gauged in measured results, and this mind-set inevitably spread into private life. Pierre helped invent the modern corporate structure, and he managed Longwood as if it were one of his companies. He set up an administrative office, kept the farm's accounts as meticulously as the company books, consulted experts when necessary, and developed a manual of procedure. Pierre's cousins and fellow company board members ran their estates much the same way, to greater and lesser degrees. At Winterthur, Henry Francis du Pont reorganized the 20 tenant farms spread over 2,000 acres into specialty operations for steer, sheep, dairy cows, poultry, pigs, vegetables, etc. His progressive agricultural experiments, especially the

INTRODUCTION

Pool house at Buena Vista designed by the Homsey office, 1937

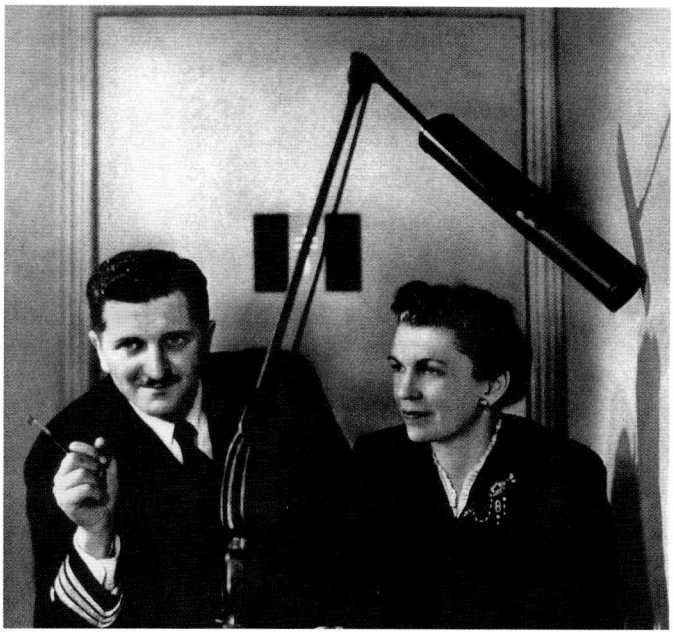

Samuel Eldon and Victorine du Pont Homsey, ca. 1942

INTRODUCTION

A. I. duPont's carillon tower under construction, October 24, 1935

INTRODUCTION

Interior of the carillon tower, which became A. I. duPont's mausoleum at his death in 1935

Holstein breeding venture, had national significance.[12] The du Ponts' attachment to the land may have been feudal, but their farming methods and treatment of their employees was rational and up to date.

The great period of du Pont family building in Wilmington coincides with the American Country Place Era (1890–1942), when middle-class and wealthy Americans put up country houses at an unprecedented rate. For the du Ponts in the Brandywine Valley, construction spiked during the Great Depression. The reasons for this expansion ranged from an increase in personal income to the emergence of a new generation (Pierre had 23 nieces and nephews marry between 1927 and 1940). The construction boom was not all new housing, however. A significant number of older du Pont houses were remodeled during the decade: Saint Amour, Winterthur, Lower Louviers, and Buena Vista. At A. I. duPont's Nemours, the gardens were expanded and a carillon tower was built. In 1938 the Delaware chapter of the American Institute of Architects, founded in 1932, reported that "many Wilmington architects are busy with commissions drawing up plans for large country estates."[13] Not every estate in Wilmington was occupied by a du Pont. Some belonged to company executives (H. G. Haskell's Hillgirt Farm and John Jacob Raskob's Archmere, now a private school, are prime examples), but the overwhelming majority were built and owned by the family.

INTRODUCTION

H. Rodney Sharp (middle right) with Frank Crowninshield (middle left) and Baron de Vaux ("Kooks") holding the parasol

As corporate cash poured in during the 1920s and 1930s, the family bought New York apartments, winter havens in Florida, New England summer cottages, and South Carolina shooting plantations, but the Brandywine continued to be home. By 1942 family members had at least 70 country houses of 20 acres or more in the Brandywine Valley.[14] The estates built in the 1930s tend to be architecturally subdued and historical in style. Steel and concrete construction prevailed as did the most technologically advanced systems possible. The houses included gardens, attached conservatories, and greenhouses as well as laboratories, workshops, stables, and dairies. These features were born of shared values. The du Ponts tended to marry people with similar interests and employ architects familiar with their needs.

Earlier in the 20th century, the family commissioned houses from a few nationally known architects: Carrère & Hastings at Nemours, 1909; Harrie T. Lindeberg at Owl's Nest, 1915; and Mellor, Meigs & Howe at Eleutherian Mills, 1923. By the 1930s, the most prominent name was that of R. Brognard Okie, a Philadelphia architect who specialized in a Pennsylvania Colonial Revival style. Okie was responsible for the major addition to, or complete construction of, six family houses between 1926 and 1940. Otherwise, the preference was for established Wilmington professionals such as E. William Martin, Clarence R. Hope, Albert Ely Ives, and Brown & Whiteside. The Philadelphia firm of DeArmand, Ashmead & Brinkley, which specialized in conservative Colonial Revival or Cotswold-style residences, worked on at least two houses for the du Ponts, as did James ("Jim") Thompson, born in Greenville, Delaware. Thompson, a childhood friend of many du Ponts, was employed by the New York firm of Holden McLaughlin. Two local companies had family members as principals: Alfred Victor du Pont at Massena & du Pont and Victorine du Pont Homsey at the firm she cofounded with her husband, Samuel Eldon Homsey.[15]

Massena & du Pont did some excellent residential work for the family (the carillon tower at Nemours and the P. S. du Pont house Bois-des-Fossés, for example), but they were not as influential or involved with as many family houses as the Homseys. The Homseys were talented, and their office was

INTRODUCTION

The garden designed by Marian Coffin for the Lammot du Pont Copelands at Mt. Cuba, ca. 1950

efficient—a great virtue to business-minded du Ponts. They were also tactful and charming, and Samuel ("Sammy") was known as the best dancer in town. Their designs can be seen today at Mt. Cuba, Longwood, and Winterthur as well as the smaller, still-private residences such as their own Tulip Hollow and the houses of Victorine's cousins at Lower Louviers, Brookdale Farm, Meown Farm, and Applecross. J. S. Cornell & Son of Philadelphia was their builder of choice, and much of their millwork was subcontracted to Wilmington-based American Car & Foundry or Wilmington Stair.[16]

Although they avoided big-name designers, the du Ponts eagerly hired famous landscape architects. The local garden competition was fierce, and standards were high. In 1929 more than 1,000 members of the Garden Club of America descended on the area to visit the du Pont gardens. The well-publicized tour was the beginning of an international horticultural reputation. In 1931 Marion Cran, a British garden writer, enthused in *Gardens in America*, "I saw a great many beautiful du Pont gardens . . . and utter a belief that no one family in America has done more for horticulture." Noel Chamberlin, who planned the Charles Schwab estate in Loretto, Pennsylvania, and worked for the Guggenheims on Long Island, was involved with at least three du Pont owners: the Simpson Deans at Old Nemours, the R. R. M. Carpenters at Wagoner's Row, and the Donald Rosses at Applecross. Thomas Sears, best known for Reynolda and Pennsbury Manor, developed the gardens for the Copelands at Mt. Cuba and the Morgans at Fair Hill. Ellen Shipman was at the height of her career when the Eugene du Ponts hired her to plan the gardens at Owl's Nest.[17] Marian Coffin's largest commission was at Winterthur, but she also designed the gardens at Gibraltar, Saint Amour, and the pool garden at Mt. Cuba. Each garden is excellent, but together they are without equal. In 1990 the American Horticultural Society gave the du Ponts an award for their contribution to American horticulture.

INTRODUCTION

The Big Bend

Philanthropy is an even more important family tradition. Alfred I. du Pont and P. S. du Pont may have been mortal enemies, but both of their estates are now open to the public, as are Winterthur, Mt. Cuba, Gibraltar, Goodstay, Eleutherian Mills, and Bellevue. With the exception of Gibraltar, each serves a purpose greater than merely preserving the founder's home: Nemours is one of the nation's largest children's health care facilities; Winterthur and Longwood are educational institutions with graduate degree programs; Bellevue is a state park; Mt. Cuba is a research center for Piedmont flora; Goodstay is a conference center for the University of Delaware; and Eleutherian Mills is part of Hagley Museum & Library, a center for business research.

Keen business instincts no doubt account for the family prosperity, but what makes the du Ponts remarkable is the endurance of their shared values. E. I.'s father, P. S. du Pont de Nemours, was a statesman and philosopher. His 1763 *Reflections on the Wealth of a Nation* argued that real wealth was in land. His descendants attest to the wisdom of this thought through their fealty to the Brandywine Valley. Two hundred years after his pamphlet was published, du Pont de Nemours's ideas seem to have found purchase in a profoundly practical institution. In 1967 his great-great-great-great-grandson George A. "Frolic" Weymouth founded the Brandywine Conservancy, which protects some 40,000 acres through conservation easements.

After World War II, du Pont estates were broken up or turned into public places, a trend at the time with big country properties all over the nation. The estate tradition continues, however, at Frolic's property, The Big Bend. Named for its situation on the Brandywine, The Big Bend is the creation of Frolic and his former wife, Ann Brelsford McCoy. It was the last new du Pont estate of the 20th century, an anachronism conceived and developed by two artists. Both Frolic and Ann are painters, as were Ann's parents, John W. McCoy and Ann Wyeth, the sister of Andrew Wyeth.

INTRODUCTION

The land at The Big Bend is showcased by an entrance drive that leads past gate posts, tenanted farm houses, and thickets of trees into a working barnyard before rising dramatically onto a high ridge with expansive views of fields, forest, and distant hills. The road dips to the river and arrows toward an austere 1750 stone farmhouse.

A meadow once encircled the house, and unfenced horses grazed at the front door. Today they are paddocked, and gardens extend out from the back patio, dividing river and house. The gardens are a series of walks through bluebell woods with a shoulder-high hedge of mallow and rows of colorful hollyhocks. An iron double staircase links the garden to the house, which is filled with natural light and ornamented with the sculptural shapes of Queen Anne furniture and evocative paintings of the Brandywine River School (Frolic is founder of the nearby Brandywine River Museum). The place is casual, with a patrician sense of fitness, including a swimming pool in the basement. Deep in the core of the estate, an open-air chapel overlooks the Brandywine.

At The Big Bend, an artist has distilled the best elements of his heritage, a modern apotheosis of all the du Pont family estates that came before. The drive is a paean to the landscape; the ancient house, restored from shambles, a testament to continuity; the garden, brilliant with flowers, an homage to a family's resilience.

Chapel overlooking the Brandywine River at The Big Bend

E. I. du Pont de Nemours Company, Board of Directors, 1943.

Family members whose houses are featured in this book are highlighted.

Portraits of past presidents (on wall), from left: **Alfred Victor du Pont** (Old Nemours), **E. I. du Pont** and **Henry du Pont** (Eleutherian Mills)

Back row: C. R. Mudge, **Eugene du Pont** (Owl's Nest), **William du Pont** (Bellevue), **L. du Pont Copeland** (Mt. Cuba), **A. Felix du Pont** (Elton), Elwyn Evans, **Eugene E. du Pont** (Dogwood), **C. H. Greenewalt** (Hod House), H. C. Haskell, **H. F. du Pont** (Winterthur and Winterthur Cottage)

Middle row: **R. R. M. Carpenter** (Dilwyne), J. B. Eliason, F. W. Pickard, E. G. Robinson, L. A. Yerkes, H. G. Haskell, A. P. Sloan Jr., F. A. Wardenburg, Fin Sparre, H. Fletcher Brown, Wm. Richter, E. B. Yancey

Seated at table: **H. B. du Pont** (H. B. du Pont house), J. W. McCoy, J. E. Crane, J. Thompson Brown, A. B. Echols, **P. S. du Pont** (Longwood), **Lammot du Pont** (Saint Amour), W. S. Carpenter Jr., **Irénée du Pont** (Granogue), W. F. Harrington, C. M. A. Stine, J. J. Raskob

THE
DU PONTS

HOUSES AND GARDENS

IN THE BRANDYWINE

1900–1951

ELEUTHERIAN MILLS

1802, renovated 1853, 1923–25

Residence of Eleuthère Irénée du Pont

Eleutherian Mills, ca. 1928. The circular drive was created during the 1923–25 renovation.

Nicolas de Molas, oil painting of Frank and Louise du Pont Crowninshield in their garden at Eleutherian Mills, 1938

THERE IS ALWAYS A STORY when something survives. The house and garden at Eleutherian Mills illustrate this principle in their opposing outcomes. The house has the cohesive storyline of a survivor: development, maturity, degradation, rescue, and resurrection. The garden's story is more common: development, maturity, destruction. What makes Eleutherian Mills a bit of a conundrum is that the house—an 1802 structure rebuilt several times in the 19th century, restored in the 1920s, and now a museum—was never more than a mildly interesting piece of architecture, albeit with sentimental value. On the other hand, the garden was considered one of most successful romantic conceits of the 20th century. Its loss is lamentable.

The name Eleutherian Mills derives from Eleuthère Irénée du Pont, founder of the DuPont Company and builder of the house.[1] The central-hall plan and symmetrical front facade are typical of the time in the Pennsylvania–Delaware region. The back, or east, side of the

ELEUTHERIAN MILLS

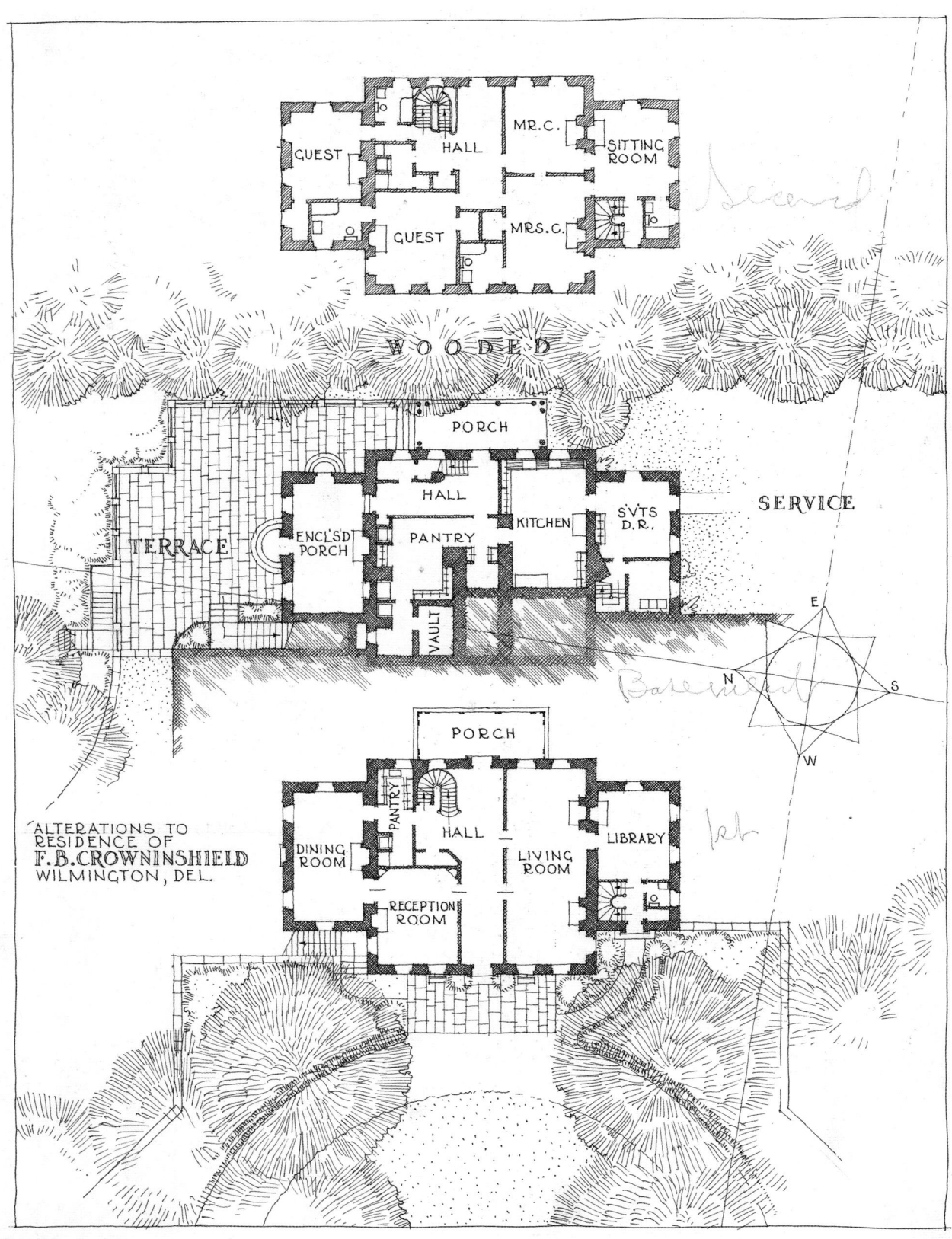

Floor plans by Mellor, Meigs & Howe, 1923 renovation

ELEUTHERIAN MILLS

Entrance hall, ca. 1928

Front parlor, ca. 1928

Dining room, ca. 1928

house is the more important orientation. The elegant, two-story colonnaded porch overlooked the Brandywine Creek and the DuPont gunpowder mills. The residence, which was owned by the company, was as physically integrated within the industrial site as the storage sheds, refineries, and workers' housing and served as a perfectly adequate, if dangerous, home throughout the 19th century. Due to its deliberate perch above the powder mills, the house was subject to regular accidental blasts. Windows were blown out, plaster fell, and doors were thrown off their hinges. Rebuilding inevitably followed. This pattern continued until October 7, 1890, when 150 pounds of gunpowder ignited, setting off a powerful detonation that severely damaged Eleutherian Mills. The disaster occurred a little more than a year after the death of Henry du Pont, a son of E. I. du Pont. "Boss Henry," as he was called, had presided over the company, the house, and the family for 39 years. In his absence, Louisa, his 73-year-old widow, chose not to rebuild. Rather, she and her youngest daughter, Evelina, moved to the nearby residence of Pelleport. The new president of the DuPont Company, Eugene du Pont, made the decision to stay in the house in which he already lived, Nemours, thus ending the almost century-long tie between the family, the house, and the factory work yards.

Eleutherian Mills remained vacant for the subsequent two years but, after stabilization, reopened as a workers' clubhouse. In 1914 there was talk of tearing the house down, but during World War I the building served as an army barracks.[2] When the powder mills closed in 1921, the house, compromised by 30 years of misuse, was offered for sale by the company, with members of the family being given first option.

For sentimental reasons I bought . . . the house built by my grandfather in 1802 where I was born and my father before me.
Henry Algernon du Pont, October 16, 1925

Colonel Henry Algernon du Pont, the eldest son of Boss Henry, lived three miles from Eleutherian Mills, at Winterthur. The Colonel, who was the family historian, purchased the

ELEUTHERIAN MILLS

Creation of the garden, ca. 1928

The Colonnade Garden, ca. 1928

Copy of the Frascati Gate installed by Frank Crowninshield in the Colonnade Garden, 1935

estate as a present for his only daughter, Louise du Pont Crowninshield. Louise, an energetic woman perhaps best known today as one of the original trustees for the National Trust for Historic Preservation, lived in Boston with her husband, Francis B. Crowninshield. In addition to the Boston townhouse, the childless couple had a summer home in Marblehead, Massachusetts, and a winter residence in Boca Grande, Florida. The Delaware property was offered to Louise by her father with the stipulation that she reside there part of the year. At the end of her life, she called his gift "one of the greatest pleasures of my life."

Eleutherian Mills was a pleasure to the Colonel as well. During the 1923–25 restoration, his chauffeur drove him almost every day to see progress on the house he began to call "the old family homestead." As keen as he was about the renovation (providing laborers from Winterthur and setting up a trust for general expenses), the octogenarian Colonel was not up to the sort of detail work involved in such a big project. Louise was absent most of the time, so the bulk of the decisions fell to Louise's brother, Henry Francis, known in the family as Harry. Harry chose architect Walter Mellor and paid for his services. Mellor, a partner in the highly regarded Philadelphia firm Mellor, Meigs & Howe, was an inspired choice for the job—he was better known for his Jacobean-Norman-style houses than those in Colonial Revival. Harry, the future founder of Winterthur Museum, had a highly developed visual sense. He must have seen through the stylistic gloss of Mellor's usual work and focused instead on his superb handling of regional materials and skill at keeping the patina of age in renovated buildings. Mellor's relationship with the family was complicated, however, by the fact that the Colonel was not fond of architects. Mellor was advised not to reveal his profession to the old man. Harry told him to pretend to be a family friend giving amateur advice.[3]

A great effort was made not to overly aggrandize the Eleutherian Mills house. The architectural footprint was untouched, and as much of the original fabric as possible was preserved. The Colonel wrote to Louise in 1924, "The two

Terrace leading from the house to the garden, ca. 1935

original marble steps, worn by the feet of so many generations of the family, are in position at the entrance door and give a certain flavor of dignity and antiquity which no modern structure could possibly have."[4] To emphasize the historic character of the house, the Colonel inset a stone plaque over the dining room door with the name of each of the owners, ending with his own. Inside, the architectural features were upgraded with fielded paneling, Federal-style fireplace surrounds, and an antique spiral staircase from a New Jersey farmhouse.

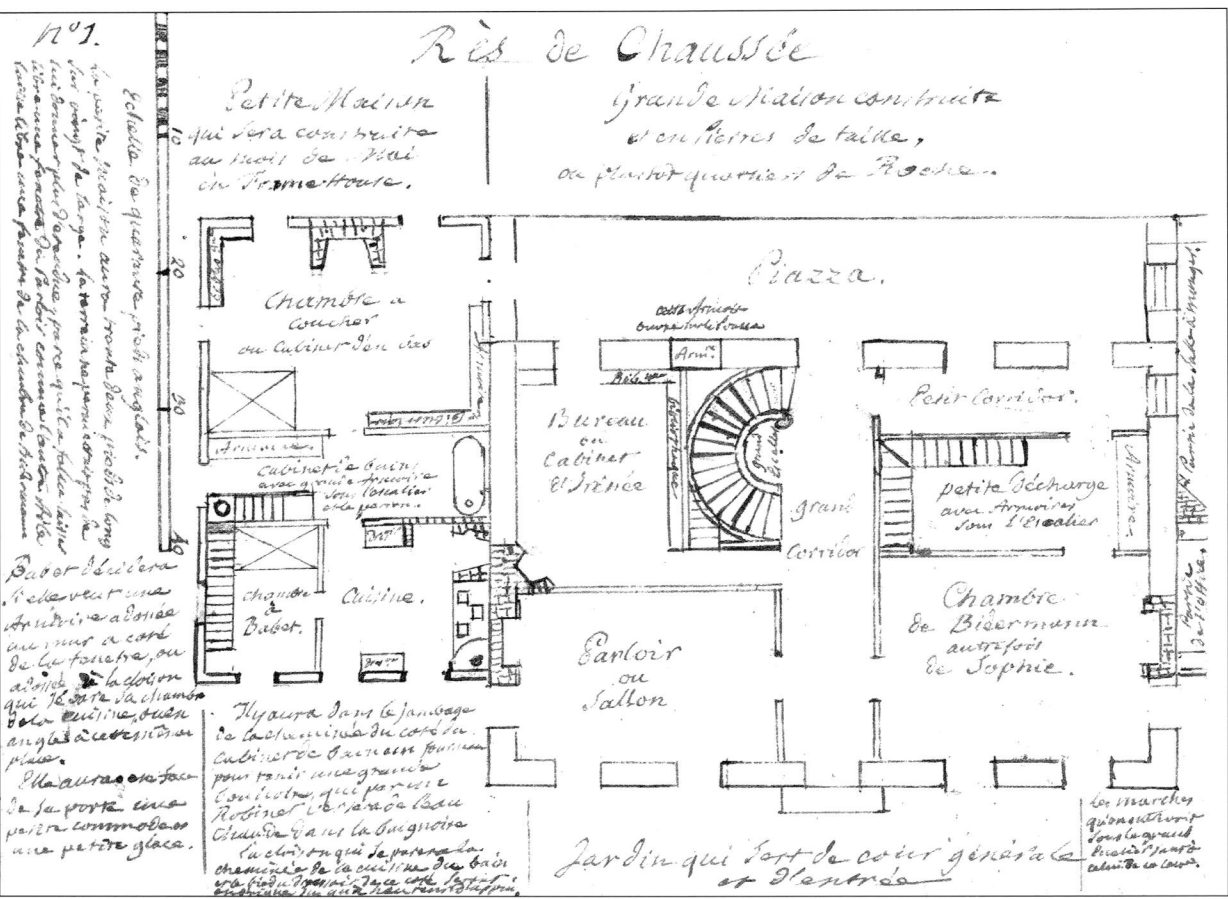

Pierre Samuel du Pont, ground floor plan, 1815

The rooms were furnished with an informal mix of Federal furniture, family portraits, and hooked rugs. Whenever possible, Louise tried to incorporate objects with an Eleutherian Mills provenance. Louise's niece Ruth Lord wrote that her aunt's passion for antiques extended to the table: "I well remember the pewter plates at lunch and the odds against getting food to one's mouth with a two-tined fork." A greenhouse and cutting garden kept the house lavishly supplied with bouquets and potted plants. "Her house was a bower!" said her cousin Catherine Irving. A staff of six women (personal maid, parlor maid, chambermaid, cook, kitchen helper, and waitress) traveled with the Crowninshields from house to house. Ruth Lord thought that the "young and pretty staff in flowered uniforms (of whom my uncle definitely approved) added to its charm." The steady breeze from the nearby Brandywine contributed to the light and airy atmosphere Louise created at Eleutherian Mills, an environment that would have been foreign to its earlier Victorian occupants. Louise liked fresh air so much that her gardener recalled, "She opened up the doors to bugs and birds."[5]

The Eleutherian Mills house came with more than 50 acres. By 1931 in excess of 100 sheep grazed on the property, and the Crowninshields proudly served their own lamb at dinner parties. The area behind the house on the slope to the river was riddled with the heavy masonry remains of the old gunpowder mills. A discussion ensued about what to do with it all soon after the Colonel acquired the property. Walter Mellor championed a naturalistic woodland setting:

Should we proceed with the development of the site of the old Powder Works into a garden, we would immediately have to consider a treatment of huge scale dimension and scale, such as the Villa d'Este. . . . I should think the better one would be of simplicity,—one back to nature . . . obliterating all the old ruins of the Powder Works.[6]

Frank Crowninshield in the garden, ca. 1930

Ignoring, or perhaps reacting to, Mellor's suggestion, the Crowninshields created the garden themselves. Eleanor Weller and Mac Griswold described the results in their book, *The Golden Age of American Gardens*: "One of the great original gardens in America and all the more unusual for being a joint effort." Using Mellor's pencil sketch of a staircase from the house as a starting point, Frank Crowninshield spent a decade developing the slope into a six-acre ruin garden. It was not quite on the scale of the Villa d'Este, but close. There was nothing comparable to it in Delaware. Mill foundations were turned into supports for classical entablatures; industrial kettles were reconceived as classical ornaments; and winding paths curved through the leveled-off former factory land, which was broken into a series of temples, grottos, pools, and fountains. Frank and a crew of masons wrestled sculpture, urns, and architectural fragments into place with cranes and muscle power, deliberately roughing them up in the process. On June 6, 1928, Ruth du Pont wrote to her mother, "We all have just returned from Louise's . . . Frank working like a beaver on the ruins. I am afraid he may overdo things in his zeal."[7] Louise planted masses of shrubs, bulbs, and wildflowers and encouraged them to spread in full naturalistic style, as if the site had gone "back to nature."

From the 1930s through the 1950s, the Crowninshields opened their remarkable garden for tours and charitable events. They hired at least two photographers to document their creation over the years, and Frank, an amateur watercolorist, painted the grounds, as did Nicolas de Molas, a Russian artist known for his stage sets and conversation pieces. But the garden was doomed. By 1960 the house had been turned into a museum of the du Pont family homestead. The modern Crowninshield ruin garden was viewed as an interloper into a historic site. Sadly, the garden area, of which only a fragment survives, is now permanently closed because of insurmountable water erosion and structural issues.

LOWER LOUVIERS

1810, renovated 1890, 1935

Residence of William Winder Laird Jr.

Henry Belin du Pont on the back porch, ca. 1900

The black gates, ca. 1930

LOUVIERS was the second of the du Pont residences to be built on the Brandywine Creek. E. I. du Pont designed the yellow stucco house in 1810 for his older brother, Victor, on the opposite side of the river from his own home, Eleutherian Mills. Twin tenanted gatehouses, possibly contemporary with the residence, protected the property. Victor was interested in the wool manufacturing business, and the name Louviers derived from a wool-manufacturing area near Rouen, France. The term was originally used just for the residence but was eventually applied to the entire 100-plus acres of du Pont land on that side of the creek. According to Henry Belin du Pont Jr., who was born at Louviers in 1898, "In the night you could hear the grind of the mill wheels." In the mid-19th century, Louviers was divided into two parts, Upper and Lower.[1] By the time Mary A. B. du Pont Laird bought Lower Louviers in 1921, the mill wheels on both sides of the creek had ceased turning.

Mary du Pont Laird purchased Louviers for her son, William Winder "Chick" Laird Jr., who was then only 11 years old. Mother and son took long walks together, and the derelict house in the woods fascinated them. Although tangled in poison ivy, the structure retained a faded grandeur. The semicircular niches flanking the front door and the elegant attenuated columns of the back porch testified to a past that echoed with stories about Marie Antoinette (in whose court Victor's wife, Gabrielle Josephine, had been raised); Thomas Jefferson (said to have helped design the house); and the Marquis de Lafayette (a friend of Victor's). The house had been severely damaged in the 1890 explosion at the powder mills, and during World War I troops were barracked there. In 1915 an explosion at the Eagle Mill caused even more damage. After the war, vandals stripped the house of doorknobs, radiators, mantels, and window sashes. Little was

Reconstruction with new kitchen wing to the right, November 30, 1935

Back facade soon after the 1935 remodeling

Front facade soon after the 1935 remodeling

salvageable in 1921. Mary Laird's daughter Rosa vividly remembered the house as "an awful place, a real mess. I couldn't imagine why anybody would want to live there!"[2]

During the 1920s, Mary Laird pruned the landscape. She found tenants for the outbuildings and generally organized the property before handing it over to her son in 1932. In 1935 Chick hired his cousin, architect Victorine du Pont, and her husband and firm partner, Samuel Homsey, to renovate the house. He intended to live there with Winnifred "Winnie" Moreton, whom he married that year. New woodwork and floors, a modern service wing, and a garage transformed the place. Although modern in its conveniences (elevator, telephone room, and multiple closets), a romantic historicism pervaded the remodeling. The exterior of the kitchen wing and garage were modeled on the Louviers gatehouses. The new wing and the original house were given a fresh coat of yellow stucco, which matched the sand gravel on the paths. An early 19th-century wrought-iron garden bench and matching chair with a history of use at Louviers were moved back to the front of the house.

The library off the living room could be reached through a "secret" passage, a swinging bookcase on the library side. A copy of the 1798 portrait of the family patriarch, Pierre Samuel du Pont de Nemours, presided over the room. No floor plans of the original Louviers survive, but the shape of the present living room probably derives from the original octagon-shaped room in that place. Many of the floorboards came from Hagley, an abandoned DuPont Company–owned house.[3]

Entrance hall with original staircase and front door, 1935

Winnie was an avid gardener and the landscape she and Chick created was as historically romantic as the house renovation. The couple fashioned two naturalistic ponds out of an earlier circular pond and created his-and-her gardens within the walls of an old stone barnyard. Both gardens were bordered with boxwood grown from cuttings at Mount Vernon. Snowdrops and wildflowers flourished in the outer areas.

The Laird property encompassed several outbuildings, including a row of surviving millworkers' houses traditionally known as Chicken Alley. At least two others had existed as well: Bedbug Row (also known as Bride's Row) and Duck Street, which the Lairds rented to their friends. The Louviers house and its dependencies are still owned by Laird descendants.

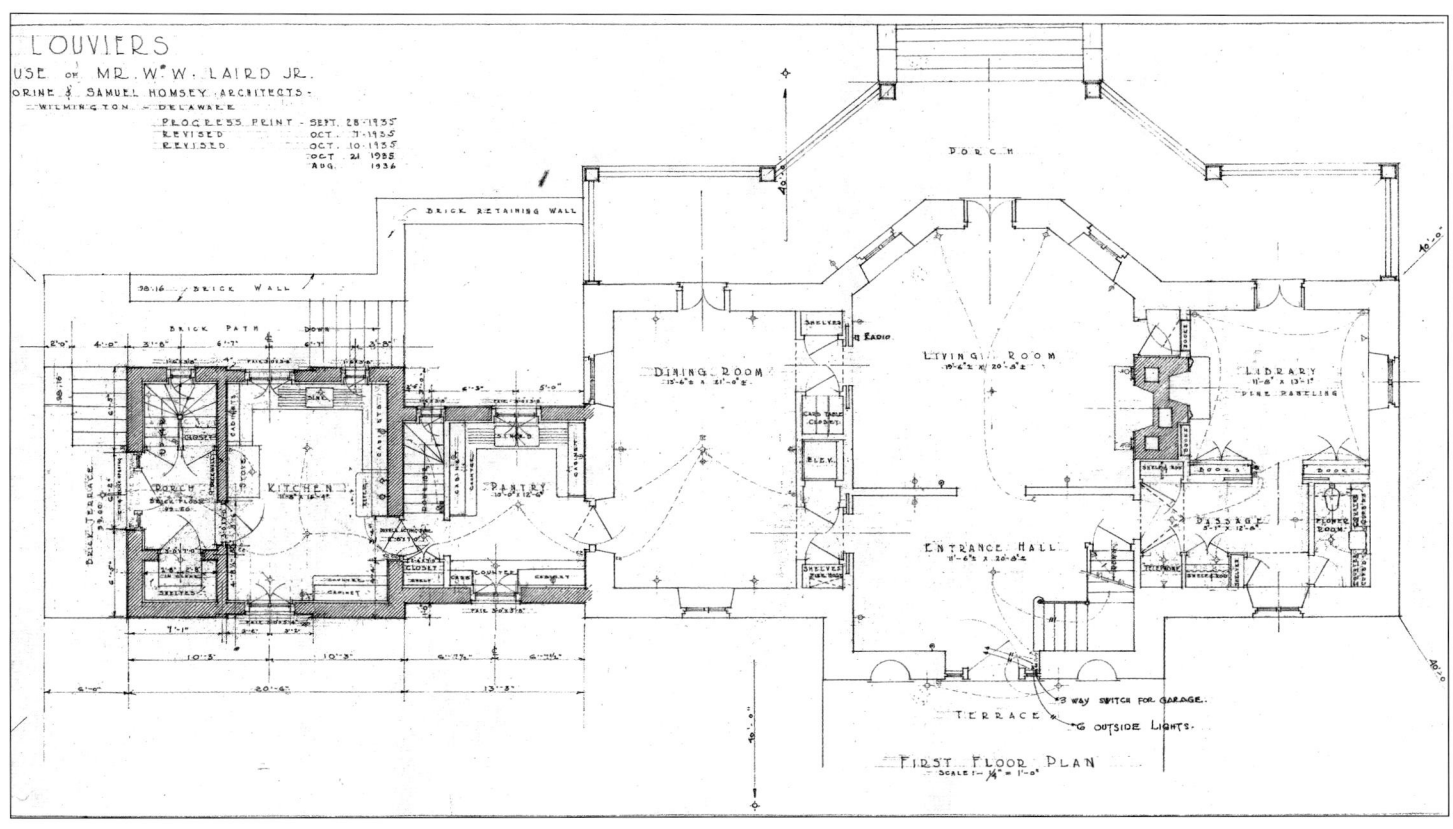
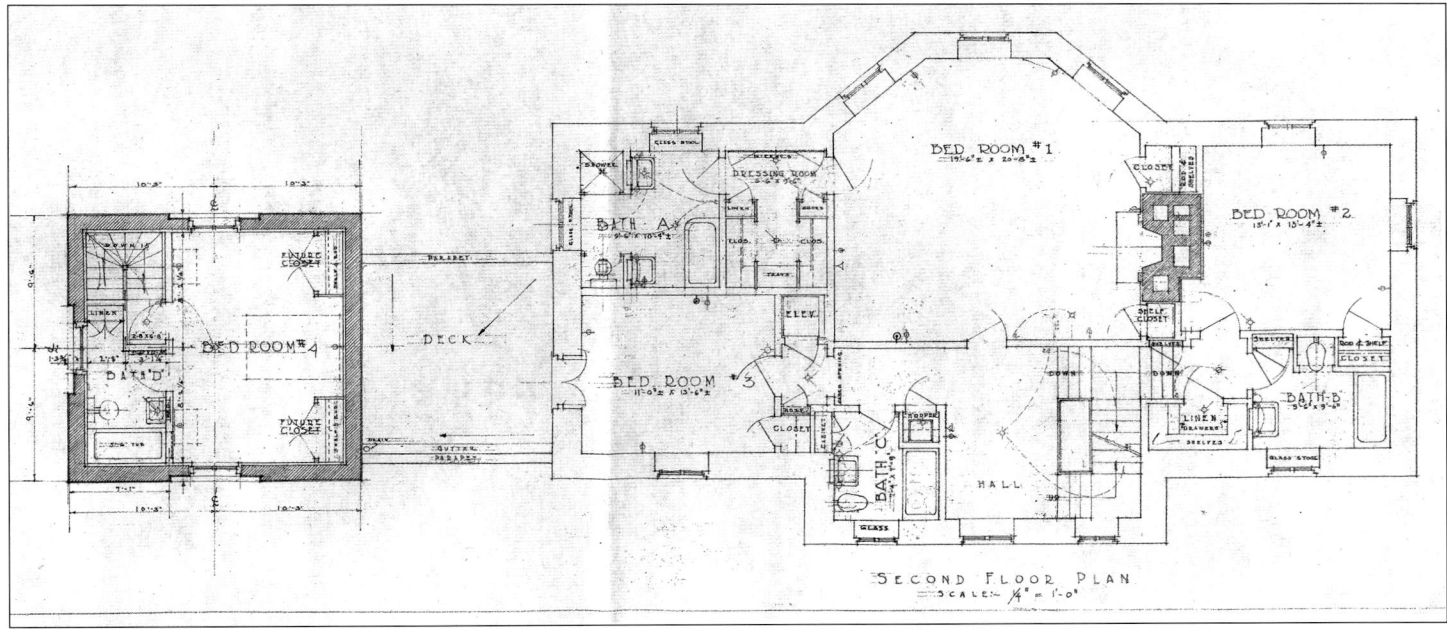

First and second floor plans, 1935

OLD NEMOURS

1824, renovated 1838, 1890

Residence of Eugene du Pont

Old Nemours, ca. 1900

Aerial view, 1933

OLD NEMOURS slipped into the 20th century as an anachronism. On January 1, 1900, more than a hundred du Ponts celebrated the centennial of the family's arrival in America. The festivities were held at Saint Amour, one of the newer, bigger houses located away from the Brandywine Creek and the dangerous powder mills. As one family member later commented: "The old family houses are in run-down condition. . . . It seems impossible to obtain tenants for them who will keep up the properties, for those with sufficient income to enable them to do so would naturally prefer better locations or object to the nearness of the powder mills."[1]

At the time, the 76-year-old Nemours was occupied by DuPont Company president Eugene du Pont. Conservative, quiet, and serious to the point of solemnity, Eugene and his wife, Amy, were well suited to the old-fashioned residence. As head of the company and double-du Ponts (Amy was his second cousin), they were conscious of keeping up family traditions. The name of the house echoes the ancient source of family pride, the 1784 patent of nobility bestowed upon Pierre Samuel du Pont by Louis XVI. The royal decree enabled du Pont and his family to display a coat of arms and add the distinguished "de Nemours" (the name of a small city near their country house in France), to the family surname.[2] Two generations of du Ponts had resided at Old Nemours before Eugene and Amy, who, models of probity, carried on living close to the factory where many relatives, including Eugene's father, had been killed.

The 1824 Nemours house was designed by Eleuthère Irénée du Pont at the time of his son Alfred Victor's marriage to Margaretta Lammot. Nemours was the third family residence near the mills. To withstand blasting shocks, E. I. built all the

Alfred Victor du Pont

houses with extra-thick walls. The original Nemours house was a classic Palladian design with a recessed center block between two supporting wings. E. I.'s death in 1834 and the subsequent settling of the will prompted a tremendous amount of building by his children between 1838 and 1844. An amateur architect, Alfred Victor oversaw many of the improvements. Because of his predilections, the closeness of the properties, and the intimacy of the occupants, the houses tended to resemble one another.[3]

At Old Nemours, Alfred Victor updated the 1824 building with, among things, a conservatory with removable glass for the summer, a new dining room, a spiral staircase, and a cast-iron columned entry porch, all in modish Greek Revival style. The porch, which casts the middle block into shadow, makes the center pediment appear to float without support. Alfred Victor added similar porches, conservatories, and curved staircases with greater success to the houses of his sisters, Evelina at Winterthur and Sophie at Upper Louviers. By the 1850s, Alfred Victor's own six-bedroom house, heated by a double-furnace system, was a model for the family and considered to be "elegant and sumptuous" with its furnishings of rosewood and mahogany.[4]

In 1867, 11 years after Alfred Victor's death, his middle son, Lammot, took over the house on his marriage to Mary Belin.[5] Eight of their 10 children were born at Old Nemours, including three who became president of the DuPont Company: Pierre Samuel, Lammot, and Irénée. Over time, the once elegant house grew increasingly threadbare. With the exception of plumbing and various repairs after the frequent explosions at the nearby powder mills, few major changes are documented after 1844. Pierre Samuel du Pont recalled, "I do not remember any repapering, inside repainting, new window hangings, or new carpeting." "Worse," he wrote, "though there were two hot air furnaces in the house, no room from garret to cellar was properly heated. . . . As I look back upon this early home it seems to me to have been designed for the maximum of discomfort and inconvenience."[6]

In 1881 Lammot and his family moved to Philadelphia. The DuPont Company mandated that Eugene, Amy, and

Alfred Victor du Pont, drawing of Old Nemours, 1838

their six children, who had been living at Lower Louviers, move into the newly vacated house. Nine years later and barely a year into Eugene's presidency of the company, a terrible explosion at the powder mills killed 12 men and demolished 50 houses. Tremors were felt 100 miles away. The devastation to Eleutherian Mills and Old Nemours was extensive. As a result, Louisa du Pont abandoned her house at Eleutherian Mills, but Eugene and Amy made the decision to repair and rebuild.

Although the redecoration was substantial, few real changes were made. The millwork around the door frames and windows was preserved. The dining room, added in 1844, appears to have its Greek Revival woodwork intact. Although the addition of bathrooms reduced the number of bedrooms by two, the footprint of the building remained essentially the same as it had been a half-century earlier. More unusual for the time are the state-of-the-art electric lights, wired from the electric plant at the DuPont Company. The glass conservatory and abundance of decorative ceramics on display contravene efforts taken against the shattering effect of more explosions. The ceilings were of sturdy painted wood rather than the more common plaster, which did not hold up well under blasting stress. To absorb shock, the pier glasses over the mantels were backed with thick mattresses.[7]

Eugene and Amy's preservationist bent can be seen in their choice of furnishings. Given their lineage and Eugene's company position, one would think family history would be on display, which it is, though not du Pont family history. Heirlooms tend to be passed along the female line. Amy's father, Charles I., was a du Pont, but her mother was Ann Ridgely, from a family prominent in Delaware since the early 1700s. Among the most conspicuous objects in the house were a set of 18th-century Philadelphia side chairs in the entrance hall and parlor. These were likely Ridgely heirlooms. The bed-

Entrance hall, 1894

room of Ann Ridgely du Pont, Eugene and Amy's eldest daughter, brimmed with Colonial and Colonial Revival pieces, including a spinning wheel, an 18th-century-style chair, and a tea table.[8]

The family's sense of tradition was also evident outside. In 1900 the flower garden had a classic Colonial Revival look, walled in and overflowing with luxuriant blooms and lush foliage. A later, 1933 aerial view shows how the house fit into the landscape. It had previously overlooked agricultural fields, but in 1933 those fields were replanted with young saplings. The thick band of trees nurtured to separate the house from the noise of the mills remained uncut. Those that had sur- rounded the house in Eugene's day were there as were the old boxwood trees said to have been grown from seed brought from France in 1824.[9] These were massed to the north of the house and on either side of the front door. The vestige of field visible in the 1933 aerial view was once part of the vast du Pont farm, which supplied food to many family members and operated around the Old Nemours property.

Under Eugene and Amy's care, the property had continued to maintain, in things large and small, the way of life that Pierre Samuel du Pont de Nemours envisioned for his family when he left France in 1799. The homestead was the center of a productive landscape, with profitable mills churning out a

Parlor, 1894

Dining room, 1894

Two views of Ann Ridgely du Pont's bedroom, January 1894

Ethel Hallock du Pont's children (Hallock, Paulina, and Wilhelmina) at Stillpond, after 1913

communal family living supported by an organized agricultural system. Pontiana, as du Pont de Nemours at one time hoped his utopian community in America would be called, lasted exactly one century. In 1902, 100 years after the company was founded, Eugene's sudden death from a bout of pneumonia precipitated a series of changes. Within the year, Amy had moved out of Nemours to Pelleport, and the DuPont Company was subsequently sold to three cousins, who shifted the focus of operations away from the Brandywine Creek.

For the next two decades, the house continued its hold on the family imagination. In 1913 Ethel Hallock du Pont, the widow of William K. du Pont, modeled her new home, Stillpond, after Old Nemours, the house where her husband had been born. Ten years later, her brother-in-law Pierre Samuel du Pont, who had written so scathingly of his childhood at Nemours, bought the house as a wedding present for his niece Paulina, Ethel and William K. du Pont's daughter "who, as a girl of sixteen, had longed to own Nemours one day." Paulina and her husband, J. Simpson Dean, subsequently turned the house into a showplace. They hired the fashionable decorator Baron Voruz de Vaux to help with the interiors and landscape architect Noel Chamberlin to lay out the gardens. Today the Old Nemours property belongs to a descendant of Alfred Victor du Pont.[10]

PELLEPORT

1881

Residence of Louisa Gerhard du Pont and Evelina du Pont

Theophilus Parsons Chandler, drawing of Pelleport, ca. 1881

Pelleport, ca. 1900

PELLEPORT was designed in 1881 as a fashionably moody and baronial residence. The original drawing by architect Theophilus Parsons Chandler shows the house as hauntingly romantic, with deerhounds gamboling on the lawn, leafless trees, and large birds flying in the sky. But the big, gray, stone pile lost its charm quickly. The ponderous architectural style combined with the unhappy histories of its successive occupants turned Pelleport into a doleful ruin long before it was torn down in 1954.

The house was built in Wilmington on a 10-acre site for Henry du Pont's youngest son, William, and William's bride and second cousin, May Lammot du Pont. May's great-grandmother was an aristocrat, Gabrielle Josephine de la Fite de Pelleport, who married Victor du Pont. The newlyweds named their house after this illustrious connection. William and May, reportedly pressured into marriage by Henry, divorced after Henry died in 1889 and promptly abandoned Pelleport. The house, complete with a stable and two tenant houses, was therefore available when William's mother, Louisa, needed a new home. She and her unmarried daughter, Evelina, were without a residence after an 1890 explosion severely damaged their own home, Eleutherian Mills. They stuffed Pelleport with all the heirlooms they could salvage and lived among a congestion of family portraits, Orientalia, and plush draperies until Louisa's death in March 1900.

The photographs show Pelleport as it looked when Louisa and Evelina lived in the 25-room house. The home was layered with objects handed down by successive family members. The front parlor held Rembrandt Peale's early 19th-century portraits of Henry's four sisters. The carved teak chair,

Front parlor with Rembrandt Peale portraits on the wall, ca. 1900

First floor hall, ca. 1900

Upstairs hallway, ca. 1900

Chinese floor vase, and scholar's stone on the mantel were souvenirs from the travels of Admiral Samuel Francis DuPont. The dining room furniture, including the sofa, had been bought in Paris in the late 1830s to furnish nearby Winterthur. The three portraits in the dining room above the sofa were also French: Pierre Samuel du Pont de Nemours as a child and grown man in addition to a portrait of his daughter-in-law Sophie Madeline, holding her oldest child, Victorine. The photograph of the hall shows the dark woodwork. The conservatory, which ran along the length of the back of the house, was crammed full of potted plants, some of which had been in the family for generations. The toy sheep in the photo had real horns from a prolific ram named Don Pedro, considered the father of the American Merino sheep. The sheep's demise in 1811 even prompted a sympathy note from Thomas Jefferson to the owner, E. I. du Pont. The bed in Louisa's room was called the Lafayette bed by the family since it was slept in by the general on his return to the United States in 1824.[1]

After Louisa's death in 1900, Evelina moved out of this mausoleum of memorabilia and built a cheerful four-square Colonial Revival house with large windows. Pelleport remained empty until 1902, when it became home to another traumatized widow. Eugene du Pont, then president of the DuPont Company, died suddenly at age 61 after a one-week illness. This tragedy threw the entire family into crisis, as it put the survival of the company in doubt. The community agitation could not have been helpful to the widow, Amy, who decided to leave her house, Old Nemours, and take up

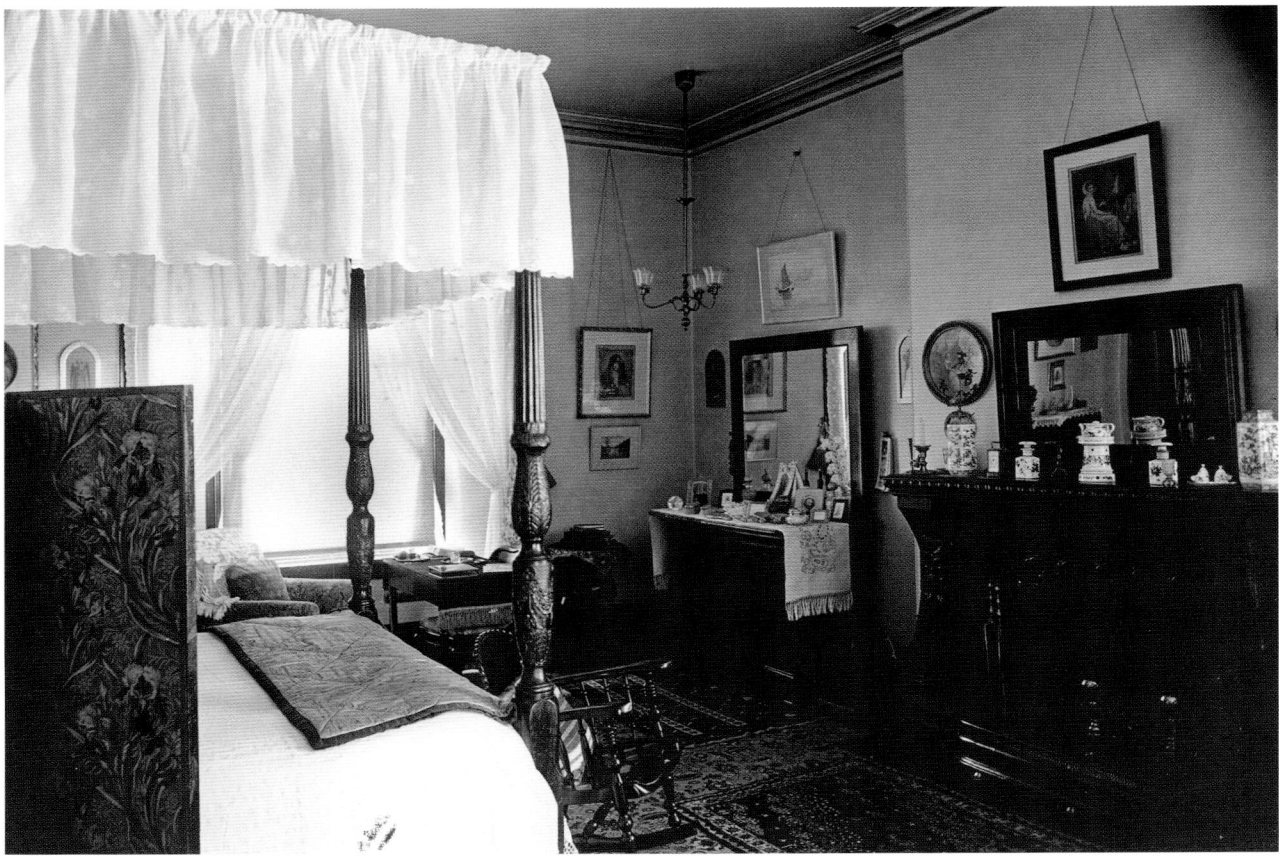
Louisa Gerhard du Pont's bedroom with Lafayette bed, ca. 1900

Evelina du Pont's bedroom, ca. 1900

Theophilus Parsons Chandler Jr., architect of Pelleport, and his wife, Sophie du Pont

residence as widow regent at Pelleport. Evelina's rather waspish sister, Victorine, wrote at the time, "I hear Mr. Perot [the architect] wants to make Cousin Amy stucco the outside of her house so as to improve its appearance, if that is possible—She will have to spend money well to make anything out of that place." Amy lived at Pelleport until she died a few days after Christmas in 1917. Her five children inherited the property but were not inclined to take it on. The house sat unoccupied for decades and went mostly unnoticed, although neighborhood children enjoyed the trick gate that opened if a bicycle ran over just the right spot. In 1954 Pelleport was razed, and the grounds were donated to Memorial Hospital for the construction of a convalescent center. Only the original stable and carriage house survive.

SAINT AMOUR

1892, renovated ca. 1920, 1934

Residence of Mary Belin du Pont

Aerial view of the house and The Neighborhood, October 31, 1927. The DuPont mills are in the upper right.

Saint Amour, ca. 1905

MARY BELIN DU PONT built Saint Amour after her husband, Lammot, died in a nitroglycerine explosion. In 1879 Lammot had resigned from the DuPont Company, moved his family to Philadelphia, and formed the Eastern Dynamite Company. The business was profitable but dangerous, and, in Lammot's case, lethal. According to the memoirs of Pierre, his eldest son, Lammot left an estate of approximately $750,000 to his wife and 10 children. After several years of mourning, Mary Belin was persuaded to move back to Wilmington. She purchased approximately 10 acres of flat farmland close to town, between the DuPont mills and Goodstay, where her 82-year-old mother-in-law, Margaretta, lived.

The house Mary Belin commissioned in 1892 was similar to other du Pont residences in the area, such as the 1878 Pelleport and the 1889 Rencourt.[1] Irregularly shaped and castlelike, the three houses were aburst with turrets, towers, chimneys, and porches. All were built of a local, dark gray stone known as Brandywine granite, which was ubiquitous on the properties. It was used for fences, stables, and outbuildings. Italian stonemasons from the family company quarried, cut, and laid it. All three houses had names that referred to French roots, but Saint Amour was a nod to the ancestral hometown of the Belins rather than the du Ponts. Mary also asserted her independence by choosing a Philadelphia architect, Albert Dilks, rather than Theophilus Parsons Chandler, Henry du Pont's son-in-law who had designed Pelleport and Rencourt.

The Dilks house was huge; the first floor alone covered 3,900 square feet. The interior was loaded with velvet portieres, satin upholstery, and enough animal pelts to conjure the popular ditty of the time: "Would you like to sin with Elinor Glyn on a tiger skin? Or would you prefer to sin on

The parlor, ca. 1900

Family and friends, ca. 1900

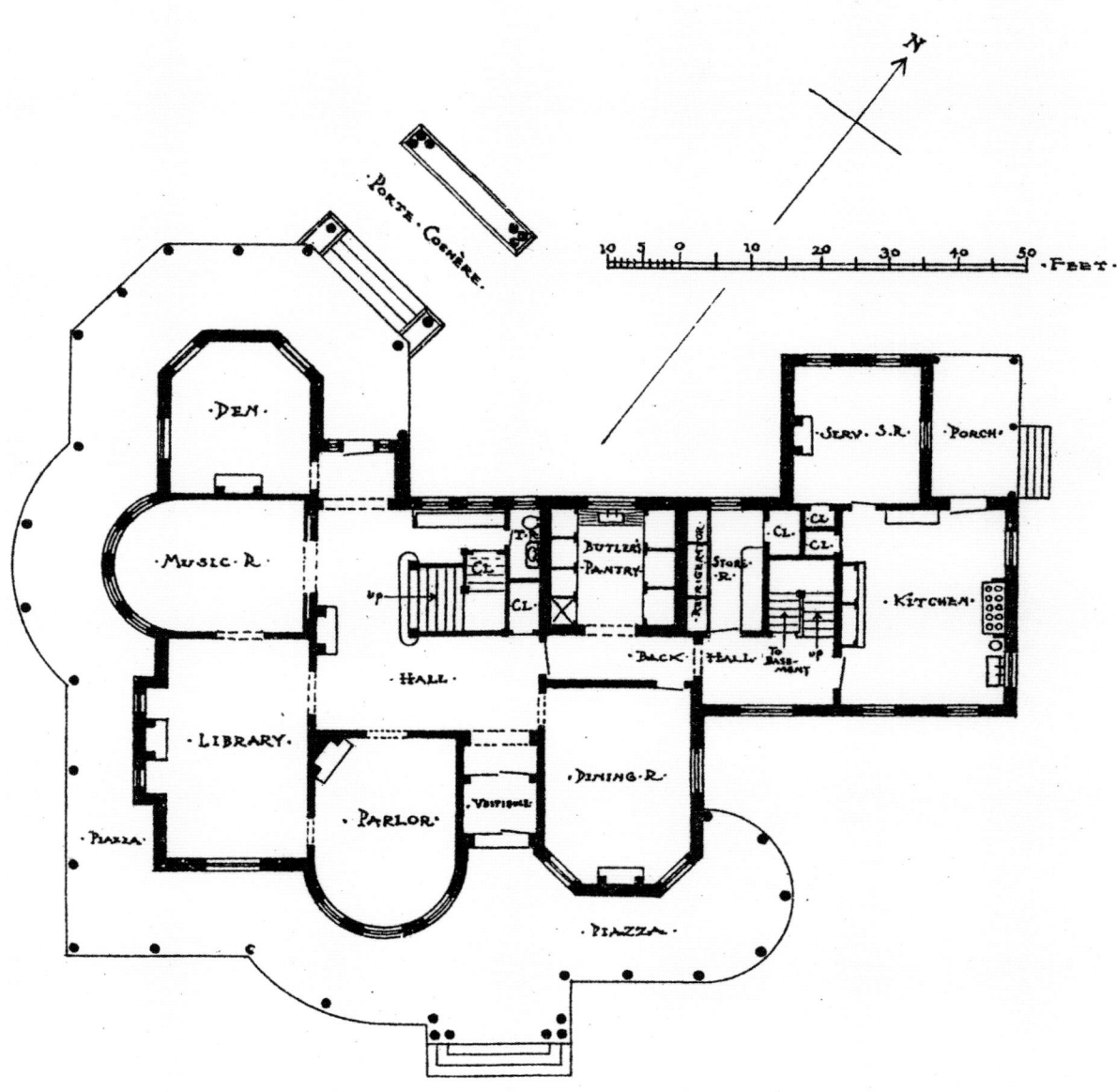

Albert Dilks, floor plan for Saint Amour

some other type of fur?" Tradition has it that Mary encouraged her children to design their own bedrooms. Over time, Saint Amour became a popular gathering place for the extended family. In 1900 the house was chosen by family consensus to host the January 1 reunion that celebrated the 100th anniversary of the du Ponts' arrival in the United States.

John Campbell of Ardmore, Pennsylvania, laid out flower beds, lawn, and 500 strawberry plants. Pierre, who later founded Longwood Gardens, was a passionate horticulturist and developed gardens and a greenhouse complex on the property for his mother. The original wooden carriage house-stable may have included a stall or two for dairy cows, but there was no farm as such attached to the property. The family would have had access to large quantities of fresh dairy products, vegetables, and meat from the DuPont farm that was part of the company as well as from Goodstay Farm.

Wisteria at the Copeland house, June 19, 1924

The Goodstay barn was within view of the front porch of Saint Amour.

As the 10 children grew older, Saint Amour became the hub of a family compound. Three of the children and one young, widowed daughter-in-law built homes nearby. On the northern end of the site was a public elementary school designed by Chandler and funded by Lammot's first cousin, Francis G. du Pont.[2] Two of Francis G.'s sons built houses on land between the school and Saint Amour. By 1916, this 100-acre block, excluding the school, contained seven du Pont family houses and was collectively called The Neighborhood. The property was pie-shaped, bounded by Rising Sun Lane, Kennett Pike, and a curving railroad spur. Each house had its own drive, garage, and ornamental and production garden. The compound had a communal swimming pool and tennis court. This generation of du Ponts re-created the company

Gardens at the Copeland house, ca. 1930

housing of the 19th century on a more luxurious scale. In some ways, the clustering was reminiscent of that associated with the Rockefellers in Pocantico Hills, New York; the Pratts in Glen Cove, Long Island; and the Pews on the Main Line outside Philadelphia.

Mary Belin du Pont died in 1913, and her son Lammot took over Saint Amour. He enlarged the house and hired Marian Coffin to design a walled formal garden in front. The firm of Lewis & Valentine relandscaped the property with full-size trees, and by the 1920s the greenhouse complex was vast, with a head-house of gray stone ornamented with a crenellated roofline. By 1927 the frame stable was replaced with a gray stone garage that matched the other buildings. The garage was anchored on both ends by tenant houses. In 1934 Lammot's cousin, architect Alfred Victor du Pont, renovated the house. He turned the old conservatory into a large room and fitted the basement with a bowling alley and badminton court. In 1969 the gigantic old stone house was finally torn down after the death of Lammot's fourth wife. The coach house and walls of the Marian Coffin garden survive.

HOUSES IN THE NEIGHBORHOOD

THE COPELAND HOUSE

The Copeland house was built for Mary Belin du Pont's eldest daughter, Louisa, on her marriage to Charles Copeland in 1904. Albert Dilks designed the gray stone Colonial Revival house and worked on the additions and alterations of 1913 and 1919. The Copelands planted extensive formal gardens

Windmar, ca. 1925

along the sides of the house, which was demolished in 1965 and rebuilt by Homsey Architects. The 1965 house is in family hands today.

WINDMAR

Windmar, set on eight acres, is the only one of the original houses in The Neighborhood to survive. It was built before 1907 for Mary Belin du Pont's second surviving daughter, Mary Alletta Belin du Pont, on her marriage to W. W. Laird in 1904. This brick, stucco, half-timbered Tudor building was different from the Colonial Revival Copeland house but had a similar boxlike shape. At Windmar the gable end faced front. The architect of Windmar is unknown, but both Dilks and Robeson Lea Perot were active architects within the du Pont family at the time. The fish-scale patterned timbers, pebble dash stucco, and leaded glass windows gave the house a distinctive and strong texture. A heated 14-car garage, framed in steel, matched the style of the house and was probably built at the same time. The back of the garage building served as a barn with separate stalls and entrances for horses and cows. The grounds included a tenant house

The Ernest du Pont house, 1992

and a large garden comprising a series of garden "rooms." In the 1930s Philadelphia architect Walter K. Durham enclosed an open porch and completed a dining room addition and kitchen wing.[3]

Ernest du Pont House

The Ernest du Pont house was probably built in 1903 when Francis G.'s son Ernest married Josephine Brinton. In 1917 architect Perot made alterations to the house, which was modified again in the late 1920s in what was considered to be a slightly racy Spanish style. This change in style is usually attributed to the influence of Ernest's second wife, Anne Thompson (1897–1969), whom he married in 1925. William Woodburn Potter was the architect, and Samuel Yellin created the ironwork.[4] There was a separate chemistry lab on the seven-acre property, a swimming pool in the basement, a five-car garage with attached apartment, and large gardens. The house was torn down in 1995, and the space is now open ground.

Elton

Elton was built for A. Felix du Pont, a son of Francis G., on his 1902 marriage to Mary Chichester. Mary kept the house after her 1937 divorce and lived there with her second husband, Dudley Clark. The residence, built around an earlier structure, was designed by Felix's brother-in-law, Robeson Lea Perot, and was published in the American Institute of Architect's *T-Square Yearbook* after a library wing, also designed by Perot, was added in 1914. The garden was exceptional, with a water lily–filled canal running alongside a

The garden at Elton, ca. 1930

The Square House, ca. 1905

long, wisteria-covered pergola. The 1929 Garden Club of America program listed William Wains as landscape architect and Mary Chichester as designer.[5] A freestanding greenhouse known as the Palm House was filled with ferns and potted plants. The house was enlarged by Homsey Architects in 1955. Elton was razed in 1969, and A. Felix du Pont Jr. built a new house, designed by Robert Raley. That residence is still owned by family members.

The Square House

The Square House was built about 1903 for Mary Belin du Pont's fourth son, Irénée, after he moved back to Wilmington with his wife (and second cousin) Irene du Pont and their growing family. Set on five acres, this relatively modest house was ostensibly designed by Robeson Lea Perot, Irene's brother-in-law, although Irénée was his own general contractor and made considerable changes during construction. In 1923 Walter S. Carpenter, the first person outside the du Pont family to be elected president of the company, purchased the Square House. The Carpenters enlarged the residence substantially and changed the name to Saint Giles.[6] In 1980 the house was replaced with the Tower Hill School athletic building.

Stillpond

Stillpond was built after 1913 for Ethel Fleet Hallock du Pont, the widow of third son, William K. du Pont. Following her husband's death, Ethel and her three children lived at Saint Amour with her mother-in-law and brother-in-law Pierre. Stillpond dates after her mother-in-law's death. Pierre and Ethel were close friends who shared an interest in horticulture. As a gift, Pierre sold Ethel just under four acres of land very close to Windmar for $10. A tiny frame house from 1877 already on the property became her gardener's cottage. Albert Dilks designed Stillpond, which was modeled on Old Nemours, the childhood home of Ethel's late husband.[7] The house was named for a children's game, "Still Pond, No More Moving." Metalsmith Samuel Yellin created elaborate gates for the house, and Ethel's four-car heated garage had a trilevel orchid house on the roof for her renowned collection. Over time she built more greenhouses. She hybridized African violets and orchids and was the first American to import tree peonies from Japan.

In the late 1920s, Albert Ely Ives added a living room wing onto the house. Although Stillpond burned to the ground in 1975, the 1877 frame house is still standing.

Mrs. William K. du Pont

808 BROOM STREET & THE OLD MILL

1890, renovated 1906–07 & Old Mill, 1909

Residence of T. Coleman du Pont

808 Broom Street before the 1906–07 addition

808 Broom Street, after the 1906-07 addition

THOMAS COLEMAN DU PONT was far more interested in real estate than architecture. After resigning from the presidency of the DuPont Company in 1915, he constructed what was then the largest office space in the world, the Equitable Building in Manhattan. Among other hotels, he owned the McAlpin and the Waldorf-Astoria in New York City; the Bellevue-Stratford in Philadelphia; and the Willard in Washington, D.C. This was the Age of the Skyscraper, but Coleman, who loved performing magic tricks, declared, "I am going to build a monument one hundred miles high and lay it on the ground." A decade before he became a U.S. senator from Delaware (1921–22, 1924–28), he was a pivotal figure in the Progressive Era's Good Roads Movement, launching the National Highway Association. In 1911 he spent $2 million of his own money to build the DuPont Highway in Delaware: "The straightest, widest, best road in the world," which connected the upper and lower ends of the state.

Between business travels and road building, Coleman circulated among three homes: one at 808 Broom Street in the city of Wilmington, where he and his wife raised five children and where he died in 1930; a country house, the Old Mill, where his wife gardened; and The Moors, an 850-acre preserve and shooting lodge in Cambridge, Maryland. In 1920 he also acquired Nevis, a Hudson River mansion associated with Alexander Hamilton.[1] In contrast to his well-known and ambitious public life, Coleman's personal life and houses were private; no contemporary interior photographs of the homes are known to exist.

808 BROOM STREET

Coleman and his wife, Alice du Pont—a third cousin who was known as Elsie—moved to 808 Broom Street in 1900.[2] The ivy-covered, brick Queen Anne–style structure was a typical city house, close to the street and other houses with an exposed side

Christmas at 808 Broom Street, 1933

The Old Mill, ca. 1920

The garden at the Old Mill, 1924

and a backyard. Elsie, a passionate gardener, civilized the perimeter of the house with rose bushes, hydrangeas, and fruit and shade trees. In 1902 it was to this house that Alfred I. du Pont rushed when he realized that he and his cousins Coleman and Pierre had a chance to take over the family business. In 1906 money from that venture finally began to materialize, and the lives of all three changed. Pierre bought Longwood; Alfred divorced his first wife; and Coleman purchased a country property and doubled the size of his house at 808 Broom Street, providing more room for Elsie, their children, and the requisite staff.

The red-brick addition was large and would have looked at the time like an update of the original house. There was a suggestion of Tudor strapwork on the back, and the front dormers and roof cornices were Georgian, but the house was more distinguished by the abundance of hygienic sleeping and sunporches than by successful architectural style. Coleman's son-in-law John Donaldson remembered 808 Broom Street as "a boy and girls' country club for his children and their many friends, with Coleman the focal point of its weekly dances." The first floor consisted of a parlor, library-music room, dining room, conservatory, and office. Upstairs were four family bedrooms, two guest rooms, a nursery, and a sewing room.[3] The house, whose closets were well stocked with silver, linen, and china, was furnished with unfashionable heirlooms, mostly Empire pieces inherited from grandparents. Riding trophies, award cups, and collections of rocks, shells, and Native American artifacts dotted the rambling house.

Drifts of daffodils, 1924

THE OLD MILL

In 1906 Coleman acquired a large tract of land west of Wilmington as a farm for himself, a "hobby-garden" for Elsie, and a recreation site for their children. In 1909–10 they built a house called the Old Mill, named after an original structure on the property. Although different in architectural style, this weekend and summer house was similar in ambience to 808 Broom Street, "an overgrown playhouse to be used for picnics, parties, and overnight junkets by his [Coleman's] children."[4]

The country residence, said to have been designed by Coleman, was made of mica-flecked brown stone that was quarried west of the building site. The structure was on the edge of a large mill pond. The front faced the water, with a narrow driveway separating the two. The first floor was actually below the level of the pond and contained gardening equipment and a hydraulic electric generating machine powered by a mill wheel. In the evenings, the house would blaze with electric light, a novelty in the country at that time. The second floor, which was below the grade of the

Coleman du Pont's camper, where he lived while building the DuPont Highway; in the backyard of 808 Broom Street, ca. 1912

road, contained an apartment for the caretaker and his family. The main room of the house, called the living room or sometimes the ballroom, was on the third level. The rustic walls were of local quartz and glittery, mica- and garnet-specked stone. Upstairs were four double bedrooms, one single bedroom, and two baths. The house had central heat, with fireplaces in every room.

Around the house and pond, over streams and hills, Elsie created a large, naturalistic garden that she called the Valley Garden. Beds of daffodils covered the hillsides, and a series of rustic bridges created viewing areas for decorative plantings along the streams. Meandering paths interspersed with sculpture led through groupings of forsythia, saucer magnolias, lilacs, and crab apples. Roses and iris added more scent and color. Henry Dubrick, the caretaker, John the gardener, and their helpers worked with Elsie on this high-maintenance landscape.

Coleman enjoyed farming and hoped to put his operation "on the same basis that an up-to-date manufacturing concern would adopt."[5] With typical ebullience, he kept buffalo and elk as well as more mundane, but still prize-winning, Holstein cows and draft horses. This fun-filled Eden lasted a little more than a decade. By 1929, when Coleman donated the Old Mill to the city of Wilmington for a much-needed reservoir, he was gravely ill and the garden was a jungle. The house was demolished in 1932, the mill pond was dammed, and most of the estate was submerged. Part of the garden was high enough in the hills to survive, and Elsie, her daughter Ellen, and Ellen's husband, landscape architect Robert Wheelwright, replanted that site. In 1943, six years after her mother's death, Ellen donated the property to the city as a public park, known today as the Valley Garden Park.

LONGWOOD

1730, renovated 1909, 1914

Residence of Pierre Samuel du Pont

Aerial view, 1927. The Peirce-du Pont House is center left, with the flower garden to the right. The dairy farm is in the upper left. The horseshoelike landmarks on the right are part of the Donald Ross–designed golf course.

Postcard of the Peirce-du Pont House, 1930s

BY 1930, LONGWOOD was one of the most unusual private residences in the United States. The owner, Pierre Samuel du Pont, was one of the richest men in the country, chairman of the board of the DuPont Company, and director of General Motors. His 926-acre estate in Pennsylvania was a surprising combination of the modest and the ambitious, much like the man himself. His residence was one of the lesser elements on the property, which was dominated by fountain gardens and greenhouses that were accessible to the public.

The modern Pierre was as much a visionary as his venerated namesake but unlike him, utterly practical. His rationality included an understanding of, and allowance for, human nature—a rare combination. These gifts were expressed in the fairness of his relations with his family, his willingness to shoulder numerous unpopular civic responsibilities, his extraordinary business leadership, and his stewardship of Longwood, one of the most outstanding public gardens.

The development of the Longwood estate began in 1906, when, to save a historic arboretum, Pierre purchased Peirce's Park and the farmland surrounding it. The property, near Kennett Square, Pennsylvania, was about 10 miles from Saint Amour, the Wilmington, Delaware, house that he shared with his mother. This real estate acquisition surprised many who knew Pierre—then a 36-year-old bachelor. The explosives company he and his cousins Alfred and Coleman ran was expanding, and there was money to spare. Although Pierre had openly disparaged the purchase of land as an investment, his acquisition can be traced to a desire to save the ancient trees and, as he explained at the time, to have "a place where I can entertain my friends."

Peirce's Park had long been open to local residents for strolling and picnicking. The Peirce family acquired the land in 1700, and from 1798 to 1880 they developed one of the finest collections of trees in the country. By the turn of the

Nicolas de Molas, watercolor of Pierre and Alice du Pont at Longwood, 1936

century, the place had fallen into disrepair. The ancient trees were about to be sold off for timber when Pierre decided to revive the estate and continue the tradition of open grounds. He renamed the homestead Longwood after a nearby Quaker meetinghouse and planted a flower garden south of the old Peirce farmhouse. The garden, which Pierre designed himself, consisted of a 600-foot herbaceous border punctuated by a central circular fountain. In 1909 this was the site of a huge party to celebrate the garden, an annual event begun that year with 400 guests.

Until his mother's death in 1913, Pierre stayed at Longwood only on weekends and during the month of June. On those occasions, he used the 1730 farmhouse as his quarters. The 2 ½-story building was a warren of small, low-ceilinged rooms, typical of other Quaker houses in the area. Pierre made few modifications until 1909, when he hired architect Albert Dilks to add a modern service wing for his staff of four. Five years later, Pierre engaged the Wilmington firm of Brown & Whiteside to build a library addition.[1] From the outside, this structure looks like a mirror image of the farmhouse. A 120-by-8-foot glassed-in conservatory connected the two red-brick buildings.

The resulting house was a personal reflection of P. S. du Pont's respect for tradition as well as his intellectual and horticultural interests. A strikingly unpretentious structure for an American millionaire of this period, it was not much larger than some of the tenant houses on the property. The conservatory was filled with conversational furniture groupings and exotic plants, and its windows lowered on pulleys into the basement, ensuring that the center of the house stayed cool and airy in the summer. Pierre was a bibliophile, and the library was the largest room in the house. Protected by an advanced fire suppression system, the space has storage areas (book, map and music cases, electric rug roller) hidden within the paneling. The map file included a deep bottom drawer where Pierre stashed toys for visiting children. The basement had an aquarium, darkroom, and bowling alley; the garage basement housed a laboratory. There were seven guest

Postcard of the conservatory and fountain gardens, 1930s

rooms, an elevator, and spacious staff quarters. Shortly after the house was completed, Pierre married his 44-year-old cousin, Alice Belin.[2]

Pierre and Alice furnished their residence with a mix of heirlooms, newly bought antiques, and reproduction Early American furniture. Inventories indicate almost every room was salted with Alice's china collection. Modern technology is evident in photos of the period: telephones, lights, clocks, and an electric call system for the servants.

Two phones can be seen in the photo of Pierre's den. Over the fireplace hangs an oil painting of Lewes Mason, his chauffeur who died in the 1918 flu epidemic and for whom Pierre named a hospital wing. The chair at the desk may be the one Pierre described in an inventory of the room: "I have spent many hard and worrying evenings in that chair, studying accounts and investments in connection with the guardianship of seven of my sisters and brothers, 1893–1905."

Alice and Pierre's bedroom suites (bedroom, dressing room, and bath) were austere, furnished with as little pomp as the housekeeper's room. Pierre slept in a sleigh bed inherited from his father. A painting of a winter scene at Longwood hung over his dresser.

With comfortable seating arrangements and careful displays, the library was the most sophisticated room in the house. The floor was embedded with planetary symbols made of precious metals, from tin and lead to gold, silver, and platinum. Some were electrical outlet covers; others were simply decorative. A portrait of Pierre's great-grandfather, E. I. du Pont, hung over the fireplace, and ancestral marble busts sat on plinths at the corners of the room. One of the wall cabinets contained a miniature Georgian dining room, created in 1935 by interior designer Baron Voruz de Vaux.[3] The tiny, elegant interior, which the du Ponts featured on their 1940 Christmas card, contrasted with the simplicity of the actual room in the old part of the house where the du Ponts took their meals.

Alice's miniature room, a fantasy of grandeur, was intended for the pleasure of others as much as for herself. The room

Conservatory in the Peirce-du Pont House, 1922

seems to be the small-scale counterpart of her husband's monumental conservatory and fountain complex. Pierre began with an orangery and exhibition hall, with adjacent growing houses for fruit. This grouping was designed by Alexander Harper, then with the firm of McKim, Mead & White. J. Walter Cope, an architect with the DuPont Engineering Company, took the two-year project and completed it in 1921. In 1923 a Cope-designed music room was added north of the exhibition hall. Five years after that, Pierre hired Wilmington architect E. William Martin to build an azalea house onto his horticultural group. A year later, yet another enhancement, a ballroom with a custom 10,010-pipe Aeolian organ, was added. It was there, amid the scent and color of the flowers, with music provided by the du Ponts' full-time organist, that the couple entertained. Outside this glass-enclosed Eden, an illuminated fountain garden propelled and recycled 10,000 gallons of water a minute. The inspirations for Pierre's 1929 hi-tech fountain were those he saw at the 1893 World's Columbian Exposition and in Europe. While visiting the Avenue of a Hundred Fountains at the Villa d'Este outside Rome, he reportedly exclaimed, "It would be nice to have something like this at home."

Throughout the Great Depression, Longwood was, as one worker described it, "an island unto itself." The self-sufficient farm operation included a dairy with prize Guernseys and enough employees to form a baseball team. At its 1929 peak, Longwood Farms employed 339 workers, a number that included the garden staff. Pierre ran the operation as he did his companies, with an emphasis on systemization, safety, and efficiency. A private boardinghouse, 100 tenant houses, a Donald Ross–designed nine-hole golf course, and tennis courts were available to the staff. It was only the labor shortages of World War II and Alice's death in 1944 that ended the idyll. In 1946 Pierre created the Longwood Foundation to take over the garden, which, along with the Peirce-du Pont House, remains open to the public today.

Pierre du Pont's den, 1948

Library, 1930

Housekeeper's room, 1930

Pierre du Pont's bedroom, 1948

Alice du Pont's miniature room, 1936

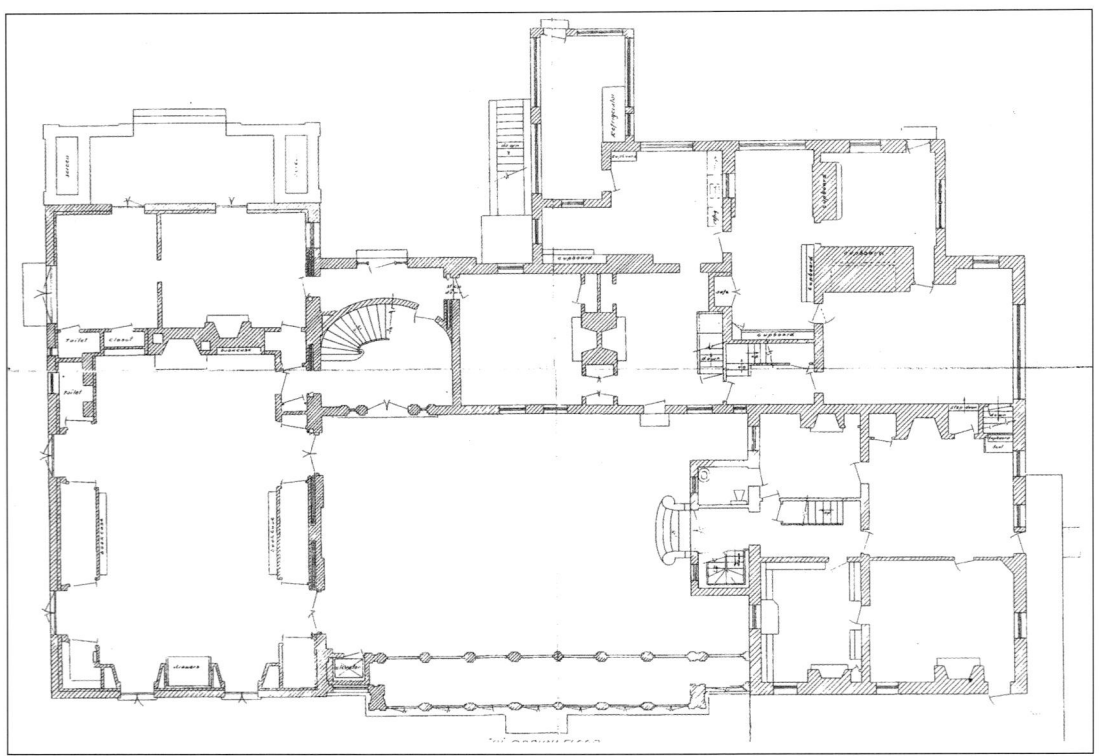
First floor plan of the Peirce-du Pont House, ca. 1950

The Centre Walk in the Longwood Conservatory, 1924

NEMOURS

1909

Residence of Alfred I. duPont

Forecourt in the 1920s

Aerial view, before 1935

IN 1909 ALFRED I. DUPONT commissioned John Carrère and Thomas Hastings to build a spectacular French-style mansion for himself and his second wife, Alicia. The date marked the end of two years of personal turmoil. In December 1907 Alfred had divorced his first wife, Bessie Gardner. Ten months later, Alicia divorced her husband, Amory Maddox, and within two weeks married Alfred. They brazened out the resulting scandal (second cousins, they endured family condemnation on both sides) by building a whipped-cream wedding cake of a house. Nothing like Alfred and Alicia's new house had ever been built in the Brandywine Valley. A century later, the opulent Nemours, now a public museum, remains unique.

If Alfred and Alicia intended to create a showplace that would illustrate their love, they could not have chosen a more apt symbol than the warship cannon that punctuated their mile-long driveway. The drive began at a gatehouse and ended at a set of princely gates that mark the beginning of the graveled forecourt of the pink stucco and limestone residence. The house was the product of a collaboration among husband, wife, and architect Hastings, who based most of the design on the Louis XVI style, a period of great significance to the family's heritage. Alfred, an engineer trained at MIT, insisted that Hastings provide identical backups for all the mechanical devices in the house. Alicia, a dedicated Francophile with a beloved apartment on the Bois de Boulogne, filled the rooms at Nemours with antiques purchased in Paris.[1]

The gardens included a terraced lawn that descended to a reflecting pool in the front of the house and side gardens of newly purchased old boxwood. Hastings described the grounds as French, formal, and big in scale. A greenhouse

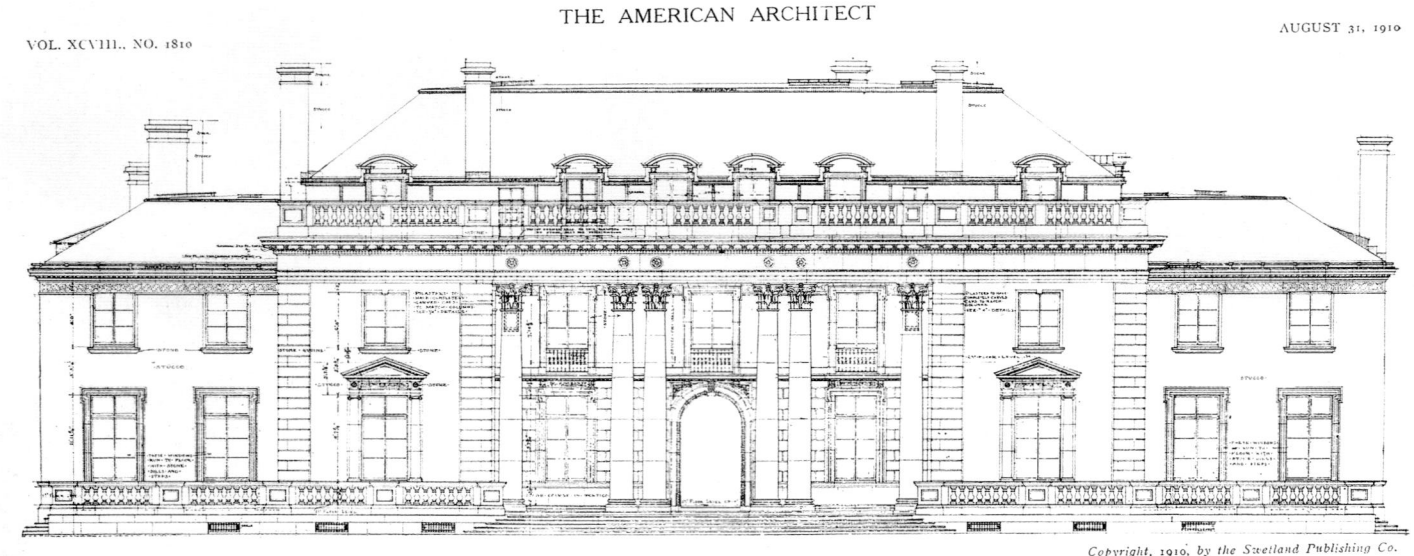

Carrère & Hastings, elevation, ca. 1910

complex, woodlots, and outlying farms with prize greyhounds and livestock (Hackney horses, Jersey cows) completed the 1,500-acre estate. The ensemble would have fit beautifully into the landscape outside New York, but in the architecturally low-key Brandywine Valley, Alfred and Alicia's dream house provoked the other duPonts, which may have been their intention. The couple increased family outrage by calling the place Nemours—the name of the family patriarch, Pierre Samuel duPont de Nemours, and the house built for Alfred's grandfather.

As the eldest son of the eldest son of the founder of the DuPont Company, Alfred was entitled to declare himself a primary heir. He saved the company in 1902, when it was announced that the family was about to sell the business. Alfred quickly assembled his cousins Pierre and Coleman, and the three joined forces and talents to buy the company and reorganize it into the one of the great American corporations of the 20th century. Alfred was the most volatile of the three partners. Devoted to Alicia, the family honor, and the manufacturing side of the business, he was also genuinely concerned with the disadvantaged in Delaware and the safety and welfare of company workers, to whom he was a hero. Alfred was also stubborn, reactive, and litigious. From the time of his marriage to Alicia up until her sudden death in 1920, he engaged in a series of highly charged lawsuits against his family, which culminated in a 1916–18 face-off with his cousin Pierre over control of the company.

In the official biography commissioned after Alfred's death in 1935, the writer acknowledged that "probably no country house of its class in America was seen by so few people." That this showplace lacked an audience was not strictly true. The August 31, 1910, issue of *American Architect* carried an elevation of the front facade and a floor plan. The June 28, 1913, issue of *Town & Country* featured three pages entitled "The Country Seat of Mr. Alfred duPont." "A Palatial Country House in Delaware: The A. I. duPont Residence" was spread over 11 pages of the October 1913 issue of *Architectural Record*. *The Spur*, a popular magazine for the horsey set, published a May 15, 1914, article on Nemours. The attention these articles drew caused Alfred to prepare a publicity release:

The property on which Nemours is situated has been in the possession of Mr. duPont's family for over one hundred years. The house contains over one hundred rooms. The furnishings are exceedingly simple and homelike, combining the delicacy of French decoration with the comfort of English homes to a remarkable extent. The principal features of the gardens are boxwood, English ivy, and Irish yews.[2]

Rear facade from garden steps, diascope, ca. 1914

Garden pool, diascope, ca. 1914

Entrance hall and staircase, ca. 1913

In these early articles on Nemours, photos show the windows of the house shielded with striped awnings. The marble-floor entry hall was fitted out with a dark coffered ceiling, stag heads, tapestries, and a three-quarter-length portrait of Alfred. The 24-by 42-foot drawing room, all glass and shadows, may be more reflective of Alicia, who had a serious interest in French culture.[3] The latticed conservatory, full of greenhouse flowers, created a transition between the garden and the interiors. The gleaming mechanical systems in the basement were photographed like prize livestock.

The house and the gardens have changed since 1914, yet the furies that surrounded the marriage of Alfred and Alicia are still visible on the site. Characteristically, the couple reacted to social ostracism by building a 9-foot-high masonry wall—topped with jagged glass—around a significant portion of their property. Alfred is said to have told his work crew: "I want a wall high enough to keep out intruders, mainly those of the name du Pont."

Alfred's third wife, Jessie Ball, helped Alfred to eventually repair the rift with his family. Jessie was a dedicated art collector and lived at Nemours from 1921 until her death in 1970. The rooms as seen today are more to her taste than to her predecessor's. In the 1930s, Alfred's son Alfred Victor, a partner in the architectural firm of Massena & du Pont, expanded the gardens,

Drawing room, ca. 1913

Library, ca. 1913

The garden, 1928–35

completing the plan originally drawn up by Hastings. The firm also built a carillon tower, where Alfred was buried in 1935.

Under the terms of Alfred's will, a children's hospital was established on the property. Designed by Massena & du Pont, the facility opened in 1940. Jessie dedicated her life to cultivating Alfred's philanthropic legacy, and thanks to her, the Alfred I. duPont Testamentary Trust is the 11th largest in the country. The Nemours Foundation, the primary beneficiary of that trust, is the nation's premier provider of health care for children. Today, the Alfred I. duPont Hospital for Children coexists on the Nemours estate with the historic duPont house, which opened to the public as a museum in 1977.

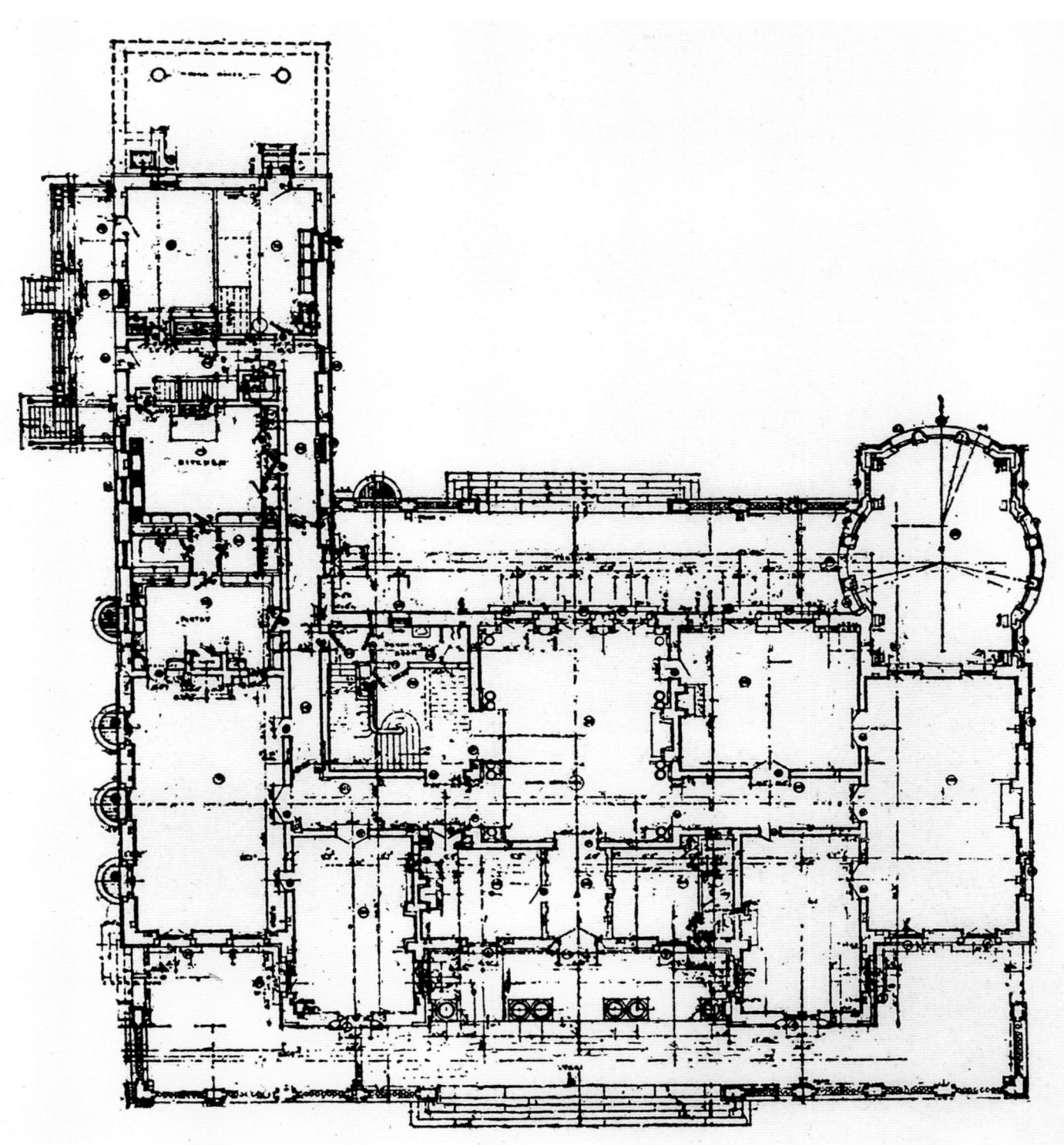

Carrère & Hastings, floor plan, ca. 1910

GIBRALTAR

1844, renovated 1915, 1927

Residence of H. Rodney and Isabella du Pont Sharp

The garden, ca. 1923

GIBRALTAR

Aerial view, 1925

GIBRALTAR was the family home of H. Rodney Sharp, his wife, Isabella du Pont, and their four children. Sharp's influence on du Pont houses and historic preservation in Delaware was enormous. He was singularly responsible for what would later become a distinctive Brandywine style: highly textured, rooted to the past, with a sophisticated sense of place.

Sharp was born on a farm in Seaford, Delaware, the poultry capital of the Mid-Atlantic. Upon graduation from Delaware College in 1900, he worked as the teacher and principal of a three-room schoolhouse in Odessa, Delaware. Three years later he moved to Wilmington and was hired as an accountant in the DuPont Company, where Pierre S. du Pont was treasurer and a director. Sharp became Pierre's right-hand man and a fixture in the social life at Pierre's home, Saint Amour. In 1908 Sharp married Pierre's sister, Isabella. The following year, the couple bought Gibraltar, not far from Saint Amour. The name derived from its rocky hilltop location. Gibraltar's six acres were dominated by a square, three-bay, stone block house. Built by the Brinckle family in 1844, the house was in the middle of what had once been a 100-acre farm. When the Sharps purchased the shrunken property, the house was dilapidated. Later in his life, Sharp remembered its having no heat, plumbing, or electricity, but he was "fascinated with the staircases . . . [and the] beautiful boxwood."[1]

GIBRALTAR

Marble stairs designed by Marian Coffin, ca. 1921

Stone bench in the garden, ca. 1921

Garden gates, ca. 1921

Isabella was not overly interested, preferring horses to horticulture, interior design, and historic preservation.

Gibraltar's stone was still available from nearby quarries, which "solved the problem for us of enlarging the house." A kind of gneiss known as Brandywine granite, the stone was used for the house additions, outbuildings, and terrace walls. In 1911 the Sharps purchased 10 acres across the street for service buildings and production gardening. By the early 1920s, at least four stone block tenant houses were erected for staff. Before World War II, sheep grazed in the pasture, and Isabella trained her horses to jump timber fences on the additional land.[2]

Sharp considered his work on Gibraltar a renovation. Although he was faithful to the heavy massing and flinty style of the Brinckle house, he completely reinvented the place. In 1914 he began the first renovation by hiring the Philadelphia architectural firm of DeArmond, Ashmead & Bickley. J. A. Bader of Wilmington was the contractor. The square house was modified to suit Sharp's taste for complicated floor plans. A library and master bedroom were added to the west of the house, and a dining room and service wing were created to the north. The tin roof was upgraded to slate, and a modern heating system, electricity, and plumbing were installed. A highly structured service building that reflected the style of the house was built onto the old stable, combining a stable-garage with a conservatory, laundry, furnace room, and staff quarters. Sharp's working relationship with interior designer Baron Voruz de

Wisteria at the front entrance, ca. 1921

Vaux began about this time. In 1919, de Vaux, then employed by Herter Looms in New York, supplied Sharp with antique garden objects. He accompanied the Sharps on an 18-month world tour in 1921 and eventually established his own Park Avenue design firm with a branch in the DuPont building in Wilmington.[3] From the 1920s through the 1950s, de Vaux sold antiques and decorative services to Sharp, P. S. du Pont, H. F. du Pont, Paulina du Pont Dean, and other family members.

In 1916 Sharp was the first in the family to hire landscape architect Marian Coffin. She divided the property in half, with a drive and park northwest of the house and a series of garden terraces to the southeast. A swimming pool surrounded by lawn and magnolias was added to one terrace, with a pool house created from the Brinckle's carriage house. The landscaping firm of Lewis & Valentine supplied full-size trees, and Samuel Yellin created the ironwork.[4] The terraces

Ann, Hugh, and Bayard Sharp in the pool at Gibraltar, ca. 1918

were linked by a curving marble staircase and led to a 200-foot bald cypress allée, which culminated in a teahouse, redesigned in Renaissance style by Coffin in 1923.

In 1927 architect Albert Ely Ives, formerly with the Addison Mizner firm in Palm Beach, completed Sharp's winter home in Boca Grande, Florida (with another landscape by Marian Coffin) and moved to Wilmington. Sharp enlisted Ives and contractor A. L. Lauritsen (whose education Sharp had paid for) to expand Gibraltar yet again. Ives extended both of the 1915 additions and altered the east and west facades to include a vestibule, enlarged service wing, and a dramatic marble-floor conservatory. Antique American paneling was put in the library. After installation, Sharp consulted with H. F. du Pont—with whom he shared a great interest in antiques and horticulture—on how to paint it. The staircase that Sharp admired when he first acquired the property remained the center of the house, although so many additions had been created around it that it was reached by a series of smaller steps. The residence had numerous level changes, similar in a way to the Colonial Revival houses Brognard Okie was building at the time. Sharp exercised a similar aesthetic on the exterior. Rather than smoothly enveloping the Brinckle house in these new additions, he chose to keep the facades irregular, with the original 1844 core visible.[5] The windows were deliberately varied: double sash, triple sash, and casement. The stylistic mishmash was held together by Sharp's flair.

Over time the garden, a romantic Beaux-Arts landscape full of sculpture, antique ironwork, and fountains, became more and more extravagant. The labor-intensive horticulture was performed by a head gardener supervising a staff of four to six. In 1931 four 16th-century Verona marble columns were pur-

The garage/greenhouse

chased from Palm Beach antiques dealer Ohan Berberyan and added to the Marian Coffin teahouse.[6]

In 1938 Sharp's attention to Gibraltar was sidetracked by a new interest—a systematic restoration of the 1770s William Corbit house in Odessa, Delaware, where he had begun his career. This interest eventually expanded to include other significant 18th-century buildings in the historic town. Despite his fascination with Odessa, his lifelong dedication to the University of Delaware, and the charms of his other houses (Eastern Shore, Maryland; Boca Grande, Florida; and Rehoboth Beach, Delaware), Gibraltar remained Sharp's primary home. In 1966, after a lifetime of philanthropic projects, he listed the "Restoration of Gibraltar and design of gardens," as his number-one interest.[7] He died in 1968 aboard ship en route from Europe, the last of more than 50 transatlantic crossings. At the service held for him in the conservatory at Gibraltar, his coffin was covered with a blanket of ivy clipped from the house. Antiques dealer J. A. Lloyd Hyde, wrote to H. F. du Pont, "All over the house were the most lovely flowers in vases . . . just as Rod used to have them himself . . . Gardenia blooms had been attached to the two large gardenia bushes flanking the front door . . . jellied soup, little sandwiches . . . it was all very well done and Rod would have approved."

Despite Sharp's stature in Delaware society, he remains an elusive figure. The arts in which he excelled—negotiation, interior design, flower arranging, and party giving—are ephemeral. No photos of the interior of Gibraltar seem to exist. Following the death of H. Rodney Sharp's son, H. Rodney Sharp Jr., in 1990, the house and property were given by the family to Preservation Delaware. Due to the importance of the Marian Coffin garden, Gibraltar is now on the National Register of Historic Places. The garden, undergoing restoration, is open to the public seven days a week.

OWL'S NEST

1917

Residence of Eugene du Pont Jr.

Main facade

Aerial view of Owl's Nest house (foreground), with farm group above, 1927

Aerial view of greenhouses, 1927

Ethel du Pont on her wedding day, June 30, 1937

OWL'S NEST became one of the most famous houses in America in 1937. On June 30 of that year, debutante Ethel du Pont married Franklin Delano Roosevelt Jr., the president's son, and the reception for 1,300 guests was held at the bride's childhood home, which appeared to be a storybook setting for romance. A thunderstorm drenched the ceremony, and political differences between the families froze the celebration, but the press duly covered the event as "the wedding of the year."

More picturesque than usual for the du Pont family, Owl's Nest still reigns as one of the most architecturally significant buildings in the Wilmington area. The swooping slate roof hallmarked the structure as the work of one of the master architects of the time, Harrie T. Lindeberg. He designed not only the Tudor-style main residence (completed in 1917) but the farm group as well—from icehouse and greenhouses to barns and tenant houses. In the late 1920s, Ellen Shipman, dubbed "the dean of American landscape architects" by *House & Garden*, collaborated with Lindeberg on the adjacent boxwood terrace garden. Louise Edey, a fashionable Park Avenue decorator, undertook the interiors.[1] Renowned metalsmith Oscar Bach, who worked on the Empire State and Chrysler buildings, created decorative details.

Owl's Nest was the home of Ethel Pyle and Eugene du Pont Jr.. Eugene, the younger son of the last head of the DuPont Company partnership, held the largest private share of

Garden off the sunroom, ca. 1930

DuPont Company stock in the 1930s. He retired in 1912 at the age of 39 and spent the rest of his life, as he later described it, "farming, fishing, and shooting." The farming took place at Owl's Nest. Agriculture was such a passion that his nickname was "Dirty Gene," partly to distinguish him from his first cousin, Eugene E. du Pont, known as "Clean Gene."

The name Owl's Nest derives from a 19th-century tavern once located at the corner of the property. Eugene bought up parts of three different farms to form the 523-acre core of his Delaware estate and embarked on experimental farming. In the 1947 Harvard yearbook, he noted that he developed his own hybrid corn to fatten his steer, pigs, and other livestock. The Lindeberg-designed barn was standard in form, using up-to-date fireproof building materials and construction techniques such as poured concrete floors and foundations. An overlay of Tudor details helped connect the barns and outbuildings to the main residence: eyebrow dormers emerged from the slate roofs; half-timbering decorated the walls; and rusticated timbers framed door and window openings.[2] On the whole, the farm group was a less successful adaptation of historic style on modern structures than the house.

The house at Owl's Nest sat on one of the highest points in Delaware, overlooking fields and forest. "The principal feature of the country house is the roof," wrote Lindeberg.[3] Irregular in shape, with multiple eaves and beautifully colored oversize slate, the roof is distinctive, and the rest of the house

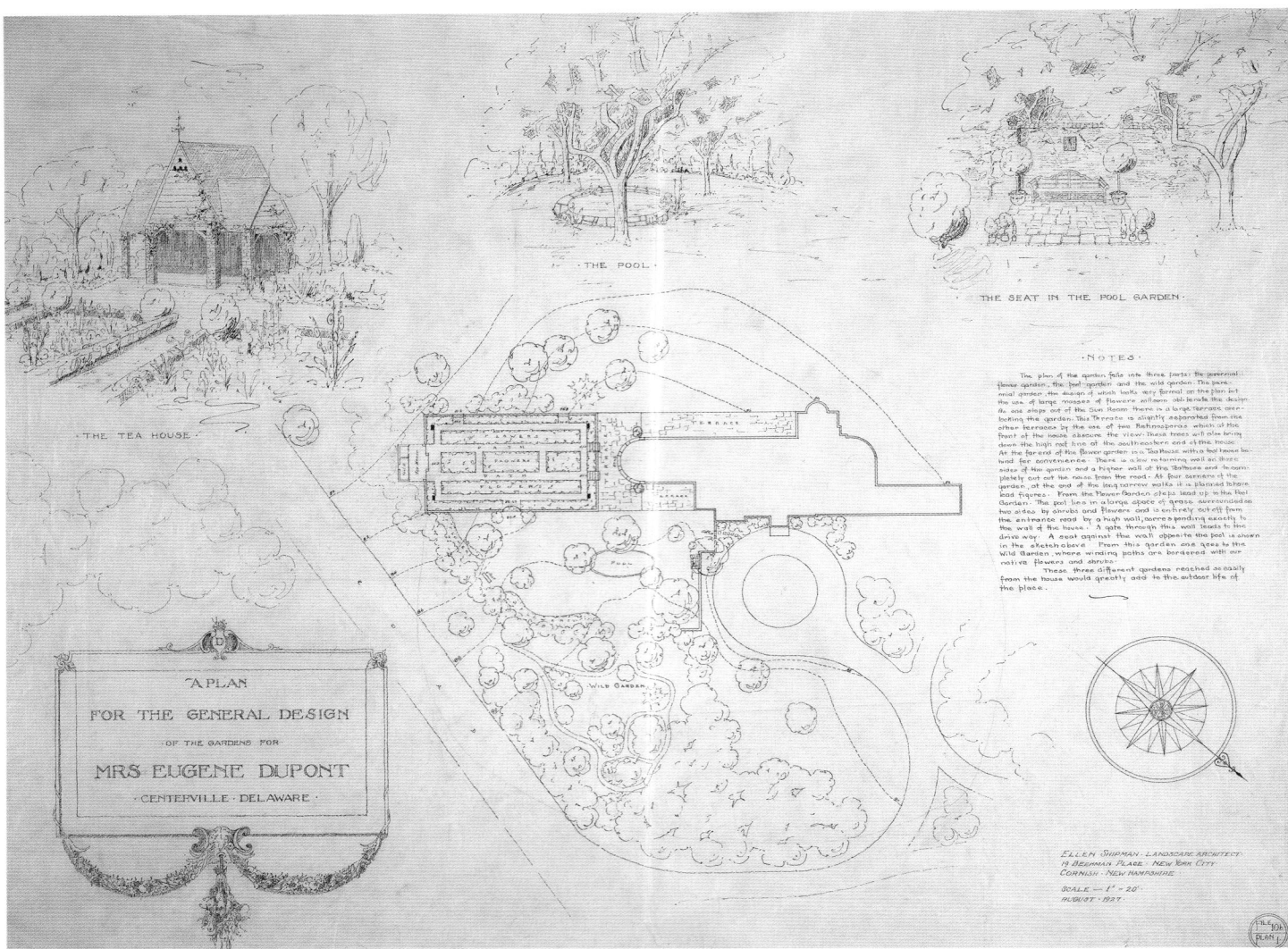

Ellen Shipman's garden plan, 1927

seemed to exist only to support the undulating crown. Burnt-face bricks and oversize chimney pots gave the house a fairy-tale quality, a feeling accentuated by Bach's copper scrollwork eagle in the door transom, elk antlers perched on one of the gables, and the oversize hammered-iron ring pull on the front door. Ivy bearded the walls, and an icehouse shaped like a dovecote enhanced the service court in back of the house.

Inside the front door, the "Olde English" atmosphere continued in the two-story galleried hall where a massive chimneypiece was carved with the du Pont family coat of arms and boxy strapwork decorated the staircase. A formal paneled living room with a Grinling Gibbons–style chimneypiece led into a modern flagstone sunroom. The dining room and marble-floor, oval-shape breakfast room had beautiful views out over the lawns and fields. Eugene and Ethel had four children, and the house was plainly built for family life, with playrooms, nurses' rooms, and children's bedrooms on the third floor, and the parents' suites and staff bedrooms on the second. Although the Eugene du Ponts socialized with a sophisticated New York-Philadelphia-Palm Beach hunt set, the guest rooms in the house were few.

By the late 1920s, a parterred flower garden, possibly developed as a cutting garden, sat next to the greenhouse, but there were no views of this area from the house. In 1927 the du Ponts commissioned Ellen Shipman to create a flower garden adjoining the

Lily pond and fountain, ca. 1930

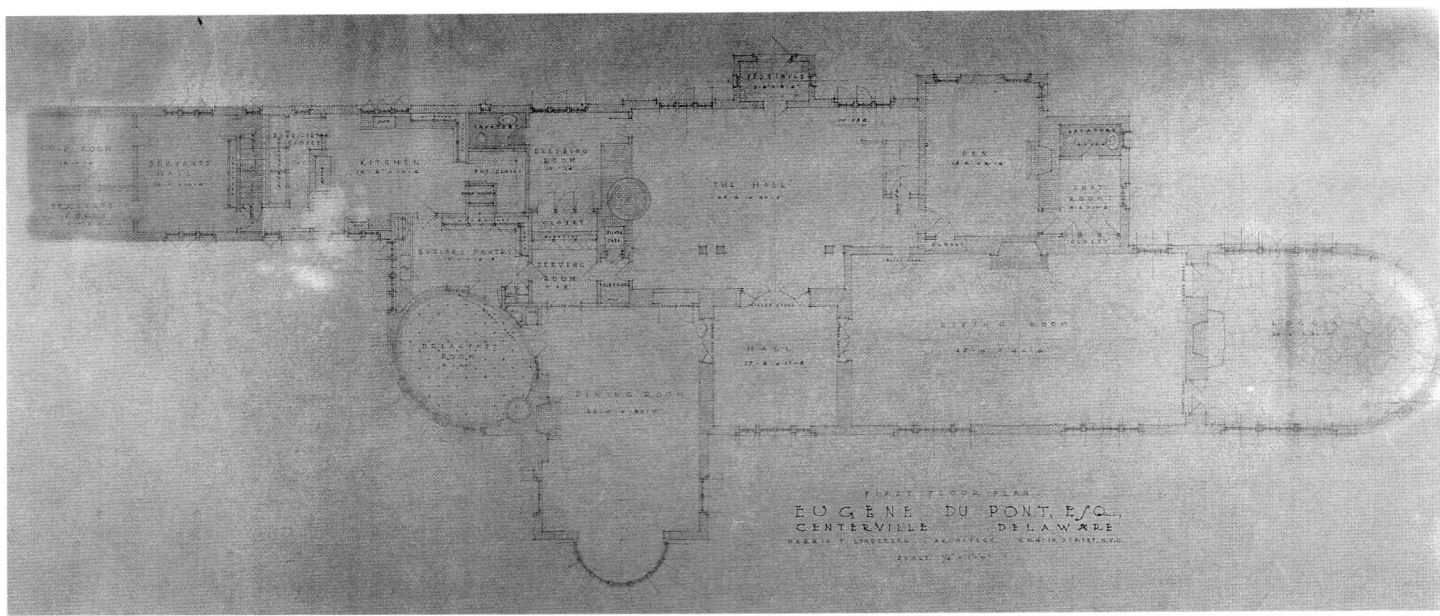

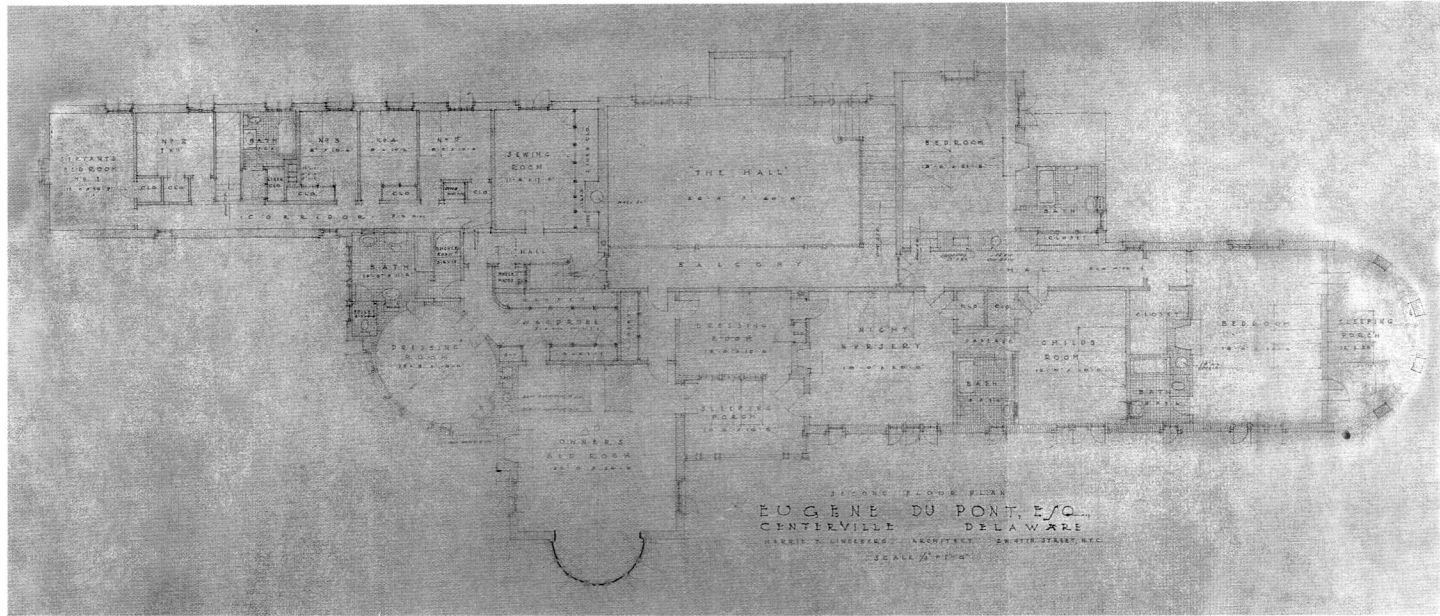

First and second floor plans, ca. 1914

sunroom. Shipman had collaborated with Lindeberg on at least two previous commissions.[4] For the du Ponts, they devised a teahouse garden scheme, with the new building facing the house. The garden between the teahouse and the sunroom formed a circle cut into quadrants, hedged in with shrubs, plots of grass, and flower beds. A small pool featuring a bubbling lotus fountain added sound and movement to the area.

The fuel shortages of the war years must have been difficult. By the time Eugene du Pont died in 1954, Owl's Nest had lost its fashionable gloss, and it sat vacant and unheated for six years before being sold in 1961 to the Greenville Country Club. The farm was divided into lots, and Owl's Nest, one of the early 20th-century du Pont estates, became the first to be broken up.

SECOND OFFICE

1872, renovated ca. 1918

Residence of E. Paul du Pont

Second Office, before 1919

SECOND OFFICE

Aerial view, April 28, 1933. The Eleutherian Mills barn is in the background.

IN JANUARY 1945 Jean Kane Foulke du Pont informed family members that she was "engaged in writing the history of the houses on the Brandywine which are occupied by family." She herself lived in one of the more distinctive houses, whose history was tightly woven into the history of the DuPont Company. Built in 1872 as a corporate office, the original structure, known as the Second Office, was not occupied until the death of then company president Henry du Pont in 1889. His successor, Eugene du Pont, did set up headquarters in the building, only a few hundred feet from his own house, Old Nemours. Following Eugene's death in 1902, the DuPont Company offices relocated to a larger space in downtown Wilmington.

After the company moved out, William K. du Pont and his family lived briefly in the Second Office. The building seemed unpromising as a residence. Constructed to withstand explosions, the dark stone block edifice was squat and heavy, covering more than 12,000 square feet.[1] Inside, high ceilings, immense rooms, and bright light from the long windows created a factory-like atmosphere. Few modifications were made before William K.'s sudden death from typhoid fever in 1907.

In 1911 E. Paul du Pont and Jean, his wife of four years, bought the Second Office. They rented out the building until 1914, when it became their residence. Years later Jean recalled that she cried for a week when she learned that the Second Office was to be their home. The major advantage of

SECOND OFFICE

Entrance hall, ca. 1920

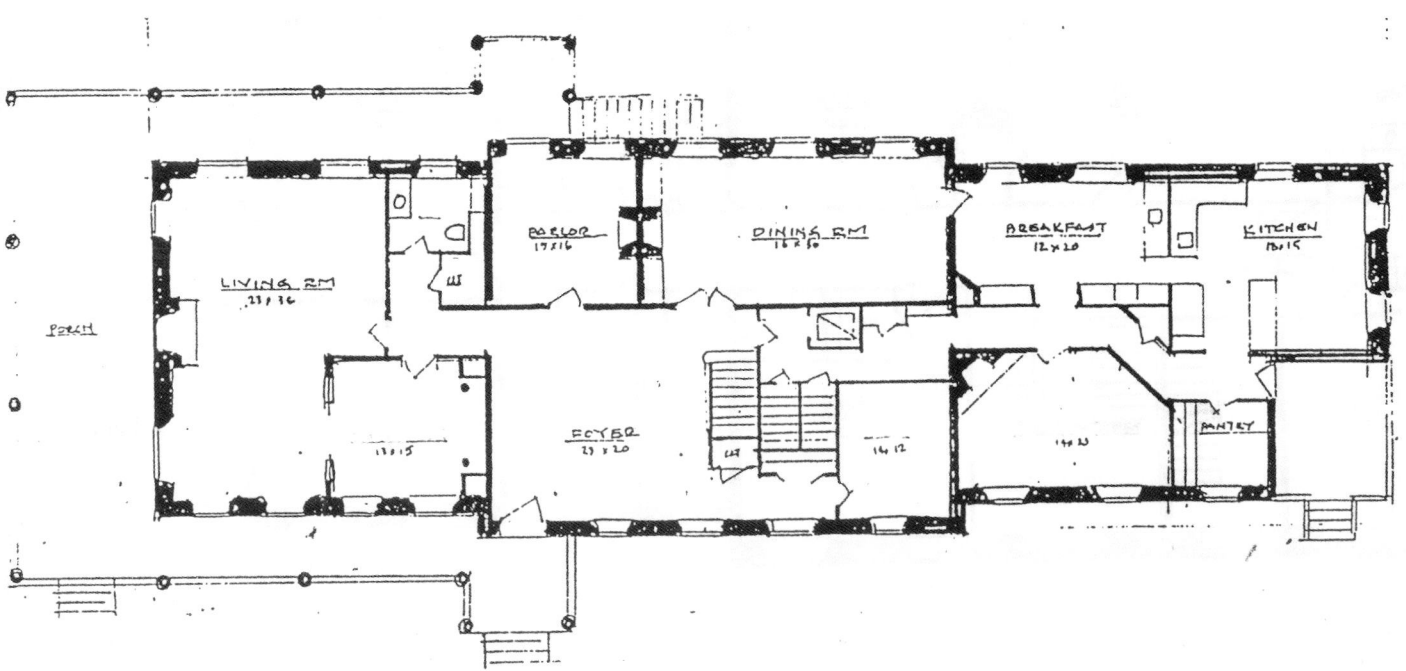

First floor plan, ca. 1985

E. Paul du Pont's Du Pont Motors car with a child's model car next to it, 1929

the building was its location, amid other family houses and near the family church. The next four years were hectic for the young couple. Jean had three sons (eventually six) and was an active suffragette who, in 1916, picketed the White House. Paul was involved in two lawsuits against the DuPont Company. In addition, World War I intervened. Paul served as a captain in the army, and Jean was deeply involved in the war effort at home. Somehow, during that turbulent time, they completely transformed the Second Office. The facade was rebuilt. The dark stone was covered in a light-color stucco; the factory windows were replaced with casement windows flanked by black wooden shutters; and Palladian windows accented the upper-story gable ends of the house. By 1919 the du Ponts lived in a modish eight-bay, two-story Colonial Revival home. A two-story porch with white columns surrounded the house on three sides, spreading out the weight of the building and giving it a hospitable and open look. Paul's brother-in-law was architect Robeson Lea Perot, and it is possible that Perot redesigned the building.[2]

A two-part Dutch door entry allowed access to the main hall, which, despite the flowers, Oriental rug, and antique furniture, retained an institutional look. This was perhaps due to the simplicity of architectural finish and oversize proportion. A portrait of Paul's grandfather, Alexis I. du Pont, hung in the middle of one wall. The most interesting feature of the 22-room, 10-bedroom house was Paul's workshop, which was prominently and deliberately positioned on the first floor between the hall and the family living room. This is where he

Jean Kane Foulke du Pont with her Du Pont Model A at the front door, 1919

developed the mechanisms for the first Du Pont automobile, a 4-cylinder Model A.

In 1919 Paul founded Du Pont Motors, which, until 1932, manufactured some of the world's most luxurious automobiles. The cars were assembled in a converted marine engine factory in Wilmington; only 547 were ever produced. In 1930 Paul acquired Indian Motorcycle Company and lost his interest in cars. He was fascinated by mechanical engineering (his sons were rumored to have been allowed to ride motorcycles inside their house). He installed a waterwheel on the 59-acre property that solved the chronic low water pressure in the house, with the excess used to keep fresh water in the family swimming pool. Jean, whose real passion in life was prison reform, helped found the family court in Delaware. She also loved flower arranging and was a founding member of the Brandywine Garden Club. To the east of the house she created a formal garden. The large south-facing production garden featured cold frames and a greenhouse.

The family lived in the Second Office until Jean's death in 1985, and the house was sold outside the family. Today the Second Office looks much as it did in 1919.

GRANOGUE

1924

Residence of Irénée du Pont

South side of the house, 1924

GRANOGUE

Aerial view, 1925

OF ALL THE DU PONT HOUSES, Granogue is the most visible to the public. Perched high on a hill encircled by a valley, the house looks like a castle from below. At the top of the hill, however, that impression dissolves. A mile-long drive leads to a square forecourt surrounded on three sides by the sprawling stone house. A painted wooden porch across the length of the eastern aspect suggests a farmhouse, diminishing the Georgian formality of the center block.

Granogue was built by Irénée du Pont, president of the DuPont Company from 1919 to 1926. Soon after succeeding to the post, Irénée decided to site a house on a 500-acre tract on the Brandywine River, about five miles north of Wilmington. The name of the estate derives from the rail station on the property. The architect was Albert H. Spahr, one of Irénée's fraternity brothers at MIT. Construction began in August 1921, and on March 3, 1923, Irénée, his wife, Irene, and their nine children (eight daughters and one son) moved into their new home.[1]

Spahr added a slate roof atop the Germantown granite exterior. The complex U-shaped structure was built with porches, sunrooms, and terraces spilling out on every side, with the south side overlooking the garden.

The north-facing entrance opened into a large paneled hall and stairwell, with the floors constructed of steel-reinforced concrete, finished in teak. Renowned Philadelphia craftsman Samuel Yellin created the wrought-iron stair rail. On the south end of the entrance hall, doors led to a tiled-floor, vaulted-ceiling conservatory, and a corridor to three rooms ran to the east. A small formal parlor with bow windows overlooked the garden on the south. Opposite the parlor, the paneled library faced the forecourt. At the end of the east corridor was the largest gathering room in the house, the oak-paneled music room. In 1924 Rembrandt Peale's 1831 portrait of E. I. du Pont presided over the room, and the furnishings included a baby grand piano, a green-lacquer phonograph player (next to the chair on the left side of the room), and an aeolian player pipe organ. In 1933 Irénée's friend Maxfield Parrish painted a mural within the tune chute, the columned opening of the organ. A staircase led down to the organ chamber, and the paneling on the south

GRANOGUE

Entrance hall, facing west, 1924

Parlor, 1924

GRANOGUE

Dining room, 1924

Music room, 1924

Children's party at Granogue, 1933

wall concealed storage space: a violin closet, music cabinet, a fold-out desk, and a telephone. The two doors on either side of the stone fireplace wall led to a glassed-in room called the arched porch because of the shape of the doors. In 1924 this room looked out onto the clay tennis court. North of the music room, with an entrance directly to the forecourt, was Irénée's museum, where his mineral collection was displayed and where his children played Ping-Pong on the long, glass-covered tables.[2] An unfinished basement space, originally designed as a billiard room, was later fitted out to test milk for the Granogue dairy. It doubled as the owner's personal chemical laboratory.

The dining room, breakfast room, and service wing were west of the entrance hall. The dining room set was the only new furniture bought for Granogue. Everything else, including the museum room, was moved from the family's old residence.[3] The tiled kitchen and pantries had glass-fronted cabinets. The butler's room, near the pantry, overlooked the forecourt, and an above-grade laundry that included washing, drying, and ironing rooms sat below the kitchen. Much of the surviving correspondence between architect and owner focuses on the modern conveniences of the house: the central vacuum, ice-making machine, ice-cream maker, elevator, chilled fur storage (never installed), electric plate warmers, and steam heat system. Eleven bedrooms and 10 baths filled the upstairs. The bank of third-floor windows on the south side of the house lit up the children's playroom. A ladder in the playroom offered access to the glass-enclosed cupola and spacious roof terrace.

"Daddy was a member of the board of directors of General Motors, with more than a mild interest in cars," according to Irénée Jr.[4] As Granogue was seven miles from the DuPont

Lower terrace rock garden, June 22, 1924

Company office, it would never have been built as a primary home for the company president before the Automobile Age. Cars were essential to the semiurban life on the property in the 1920s and 1930s, and motor vehicles of all kinds figure prominently in the family's home movies and stories. A two-story, 12-car garage with an attached dwelling for the head chauffeur was located a half-mile from the main house, and two bungalows were built nearby for the chauffeur's staff. A road system connected the house with various parts of the estate: a post office-train station; paint, carpenter, and blacksmith shops; two functioning water towers (one with a 100,000-gallon steel tank); and stables, farm, and dairy. There were hogs, mules, steer, and poultry. Milk from the dairy was sold off the property. At the height of its operation in the 1920s and 1930s, six men, plus seasonal employees, worked on the farm. A farm manager oversaw them, and he in turn was supervised by Irénée's secretary. There were 14 employee houses, plus a boardinghouse for unmarried farmworkers.

The garden was Irene du Pont's territory. An amateur painter with an art studio on the property, Irene sketched out the paths, walls, and fountains for the garden while the house was being built. A DuPont Company engineer in charge of construction followed her designs, which ranged from a naturalistic rock garden south of the house down a terrace to a formal triple-parterre garden with a pool. A long path that descended the hill led to a greenhouse full of orchids and gardenias, with two orange trees said to have grown from the blossoms in Irene's bridal bouquet. The head gardener and his assistant supervised up to nine men who worked in the orchards, vegetable garden, flower gardens, and greenhouses.

In 1926 Irénée resigned as president of the DuPont Company. While on vacation in Cuba, he became enchanted by the island and by 1928 had begun to develop a Cuban estate called Xanadu. He spent about three months a year there until the Cuban government expropriated the property in 1961.

Irénée and Irene's daughters were married at Granogue, and their son and his wife live there today.

CHEVANNES

ca. 1926

Residence of Bessie G. du Pont

Albert Ely Ives, drawing of Chevannes, ca. 1926

Watercolor of the garden facade of Bois-des-Fossés, France, 1800s

CHEVANNES was born of a messy emotional triangle. In 1910 Bessie G. du Pont, the first wife of Alfred I. duPont, was left homeless when Alfred razed Swamp Hall, the house where she had been living. A rambling Victorian frame house near the DuPont Company mills, Swamp Hall was Alfred's childhood home, and he and Bessie lived there during their 19-year marriage. After their divorce in 1906, Bessie stayed on with her four children. In 1910 she was abruptly informed that the house would be torn down within a week and so moved to downtown Wilmington, where she rented a much smaller dwelling.

In 1926 Pierre Samuel du Pont—Alfred's first cousin, former business partner, and adversary—came to her rescue. Bessie had just completed an 11-volume work entitled *Life of Eleuthère Irénée du Pont from Contemporary Correspondence*, a project she had undertaken at Pierre's suggestion. In gratitude, Pierre offered to build Bessie a house.

Bessie modeled Pierre's gift of a house on Bois-des-Fossés, the ancestral farm home of the du Pont family in France. She named her new residence Chevannes, after the village not far from Bois-des-Fossés. Her choice made a public statement about the centrality of her role in the family and her feelings about the name and architectural style of her former husband's estate. Wilmingtonians were amused that the warfare between Alfred and Bessie, officially carried out in the courtroom, had now moved into the landscape. Pierre's role in the fracas was also a source of considerable delight.

Pierre purchased a 7.6-acre piece of land for Bessie from Evelina du Pont and then handed the project of supervising the construction of the house to H. Rodney Sharp, his right-hand man and brother-in-law. Sharp was completing a winter home in Boca Grande, Florida, at the same time and recommended his architect, Albert Ely Ives, to Pierre and Bessie.

At the start of the project, Sharp sent Ives a copy of the first volume of Bessie's book, because the frontispiece featured a modern painting of Bois-des-Fossés by Stanley Arthurs. Ives was instructed to design the house based on this image, and

Chevannes, ca. 1929

the two-story building, completed in the spring of 1928, was closely modeled on the original. Chevannes had a stuccoed exterior with limestone trim, red-tile roof, and casement windows framed by black shutters. A flat-roof porch topped the triple-arch entry of the central block. The tower and service wings, in contrast to Bois-des-Fossés, were set at a right angle to form a service court in back and entry court in front. The garden facade, which was along the library, was as close to the original as possible, although with the thoughtful adaptation of a canvas awning for the pent eave, which better suited the humid Delaware summers.

While the house was under construction, Bessie toured France and shopped for her new home. She shipped brass hardware, lighting fixtures, parquet floors, and mantels to Wilmington. She also made a pilgrimage to Bois-des-Fossés, where she collected chestnuts to plant upon her return. The seedlings were added to a landscape treatment already in progress. Full-size European lindens, boxwood, magnolias, and horse chestnuts were trucked to Chevannes and installed around the house by Lewis & Valentine, the prominent New York landscape firm.

H. Rodney Sharp had as much influence on the house design as did Bessie. In addition to choosing the architect and making all the on-site decisions as construction proceeded, he overruled her on several key decisions, such as the use of casement windows, which she disliked. Sharp was adamant that the house not be of "the ordinary type of going into a front hall and seeing rooms on either side of the front door." The result was an L-shape floor plan that maximized views out to the garden and grounds. The entry block, including a hall, oval staircase, and long dining room, was flanked on the right by family rooms (library and study on the first floor, and bedrooms on the second) and on the left by a projecting tower and service wing.

Stanley Arthurs, painting of Bois-des-Fossés, France, ca. 1925

The largest room in the house was the library, which was fully paneled in Empire-style woodwork. A secret door disguised as a bookcase delighted every generation of occupants. The Stanley Arthurs painting of Bois-des-Fossés that inspired the house was given a place of honor over the mantel. Bessie's writing room next door was a classically conceived French cabinet with mirror-and-glass paneled doors and north light.

Pierre du Pont took particular interest in the service areas, which formed a full 50 percent of the house. He argued with Ives over the type of flooring in the laundry and insisted that the back stairs be lit with a window, that the maid's closet in the kitchen have a ventilator for odors, and that the pantry contain a plate warmer. Although the house was historical in style, all the latest conveniences were installed, including an elevator, towel warmers in the bathrooms, gas and oil pumps near the garage, and French-style telephones. The service courtyard was accentuated with a storehouse that Ives described as "an attractive outbuilding, it will have nice shadows and reveals a good-looking roof."[1]

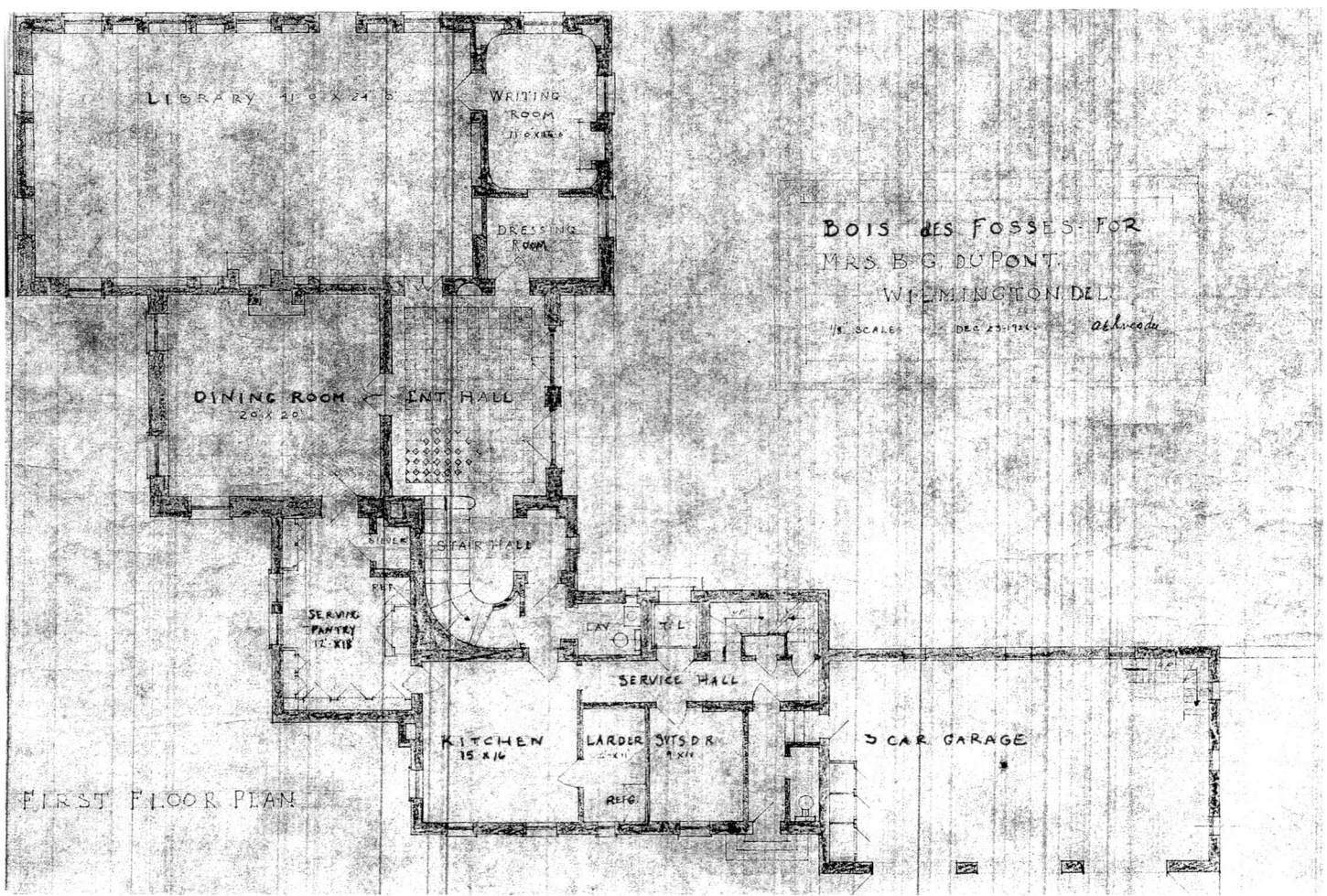

First floor plan, December 1926

Albert Ely Ives's ability to focus on the aesthetic outcome of the house and his good-humored flexibility in working for three strong personalities proved his making as an architect. Chevannes was Ives's first commission in Delaware. Between 1927, when he opened an architectural office in the DuPont building, and 1935, when he left for Europe, Ives designed about a dozen buildings around Wilmington, including Winterthur and the Sigma Nu Fraternity house at the University of Delaware in Newark. All his houses remain grounded in a restrained historicism, a strict attention to detail, and careful integration of the house—which was usually irregular in shape—into the landscape of the area. A. L. Lauritsen, a local builder whose education was funded by Sharp, was charged with the actual construction of Chevannes as well as almost all of Ives's projects in Wilmington. As soon as Lauritsen and Ives completed Chevannes, they began working across the street with Henry Francis du Pont on the more complex job at Winterthur. After Bessie du Pont's death in 1950, her house was sold to Frederick George Isaac Singer, grandson of the founder of the Singer Sewing Machine Company. The house is still called Chevannes.

BOXWOOD

1928

Residence of George P. and Natalie du Pont Edmonds

The entrance to Boxwood, 1928

The garden at Boxwood, 1928

IN 1931 NATALIE DU PONT and her husband, George P. Edmonds, purchased a 10-bedroom house in Wilmington's exclusive Westover Hills neighborhood. The 1928 Georgian-style residence, designed by the Philadelphia firm of Wallace & Warner, had been intended for F. B. Davis Jr., a DuPont Company executive. Before moving in, however, Davis left Wilmington for New York to run U.S. Rubber, making him one of the highest paid businessmen in the United States.

The house was set on 20 acres, the largest lot in Westover Hills, a 600-acre development started by William du Pont Jr. in 1926. Most people did not have Davis's good fortune in the early 1930s, and the neighborhood was nicknamed "Unpaid Bills." The partially furnished Davis house stood empty until the Edmonds moved in and named the property Boxwood. They kept the Davis furniture. The outbuildings included greenhouses and a heated four-car garage with chauffeur's apartment. A terraced boxwood garden built on the foundations of an old barn ornamented the back of the house, and an apple orchard was cultivated along the driveway.

Perhaps the most notable feature of Boxwood was the basement, which was designed as a cobblestone street lined with cottages, one of which contained what the family called an English pub. The room had exposed rough-hewn beam ceilings, stone floors, and a built-in bar. Electric lanterns hung from the

Entrance hall, 1928

Entrance hall from dining room, 1928

ceiling; pewter tankards and chargers enhanced the gleam; Windsor chairs and tavern tables increased the old-timey atmosphere. This theatrical conceit was one of many such rooms built in homes during the Prohibition Era, from 1920 to 1933. One unintended irony of the 18th Amendment to the Constitution was that hard spirits became fashionable. The "cocktail hour" denoted a particular time of day and the "cocktail party" a form of chic entertainment. There were designated drinking rooms in private houses before Prohibition, but they tended to be for men only, much like taverns. During Prohibition, it became acceptable for women to drink with men. Settings such as those in the Edmonds home added a little fizz to the fun.

After the death of George Edmonds in 1994 the house and surrounding grounds were sold, and the acreage was broken into smaller lots. Boxwood survives as a private residence.

The basement with cobblestone "street," 1928

The basement pub, 1928

BOXWOOD

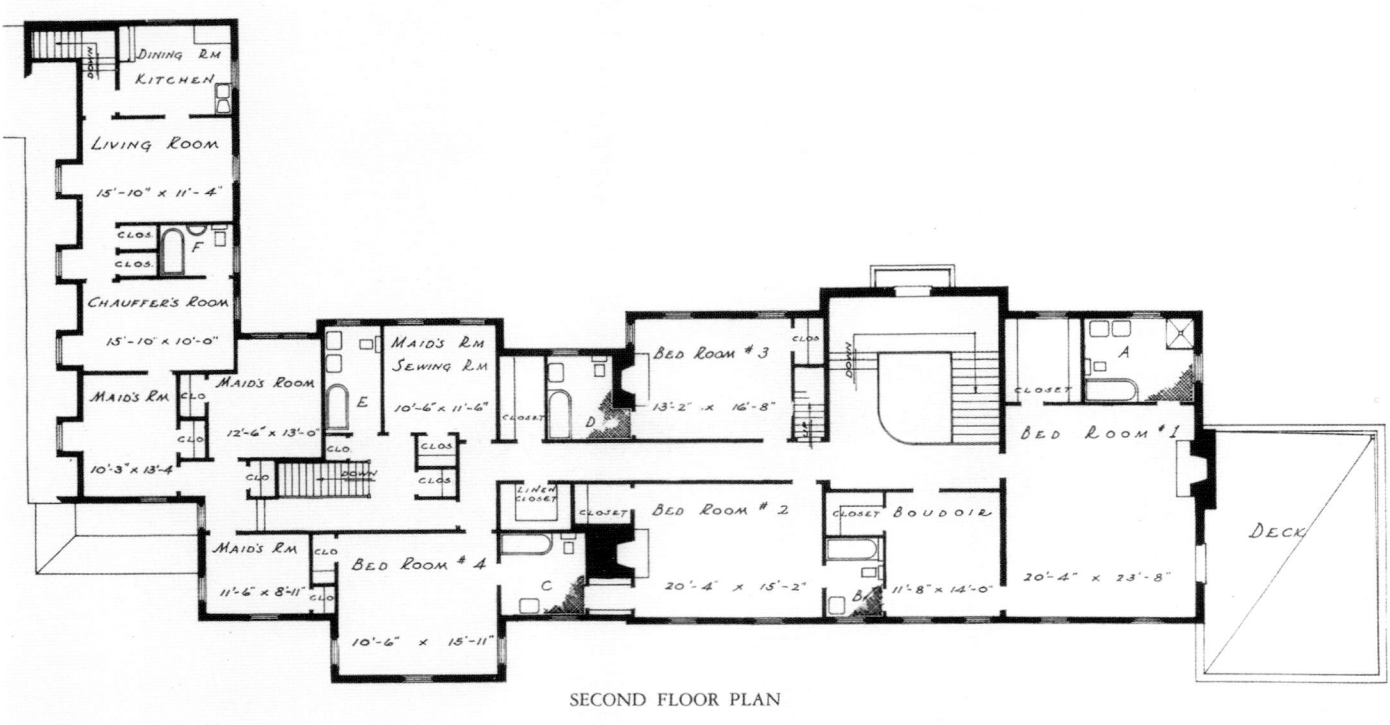

SECOND FLOOR PLAN

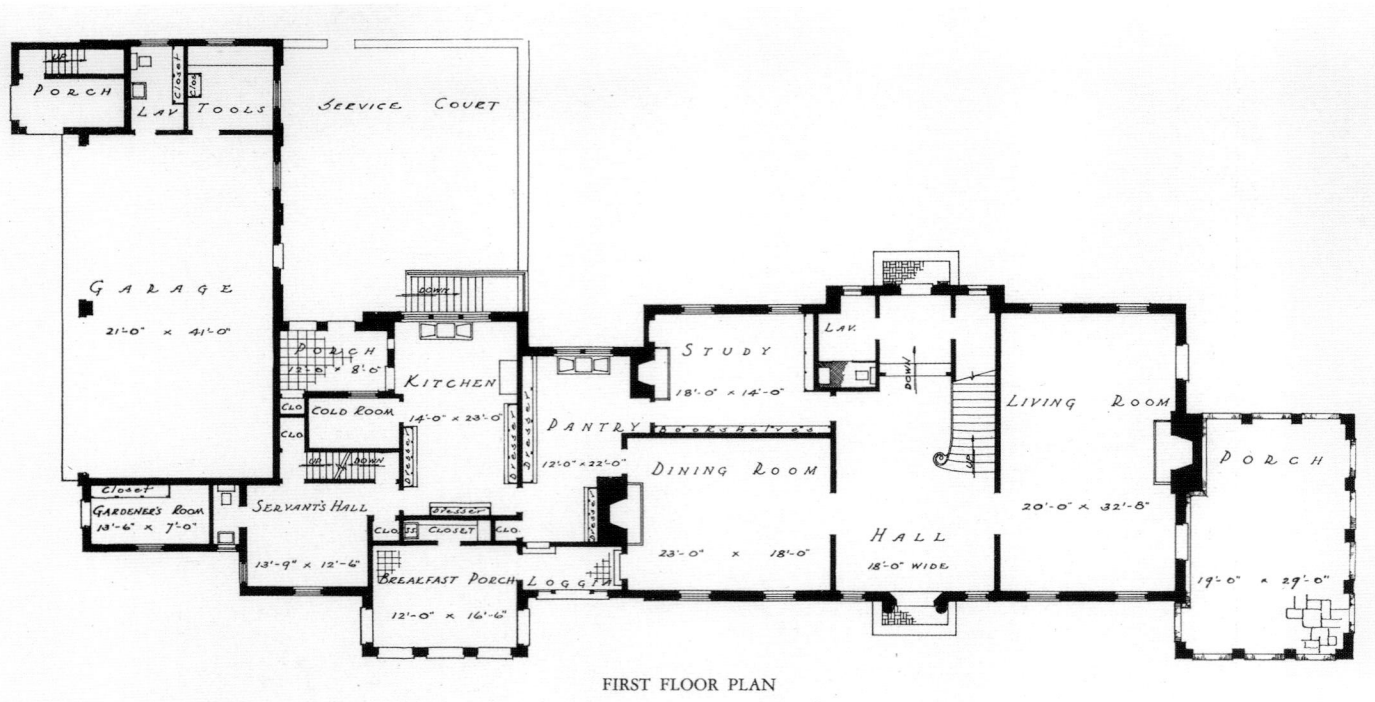

FIRST FLOOR PLAN

PLANS OF RESIDENCE OF · MR. F. B. DAVIS, JR. · WILMINGTON, DEL.

First and second floor plans, 1928

WINTERTHUR
1839, renovated 1902, 1929–31

Residence of Henry Francis du Pont

Port Royal entrance, ca. 1931

North side of the house at the start of the transformation, July 1929

North side of the house, August 1929

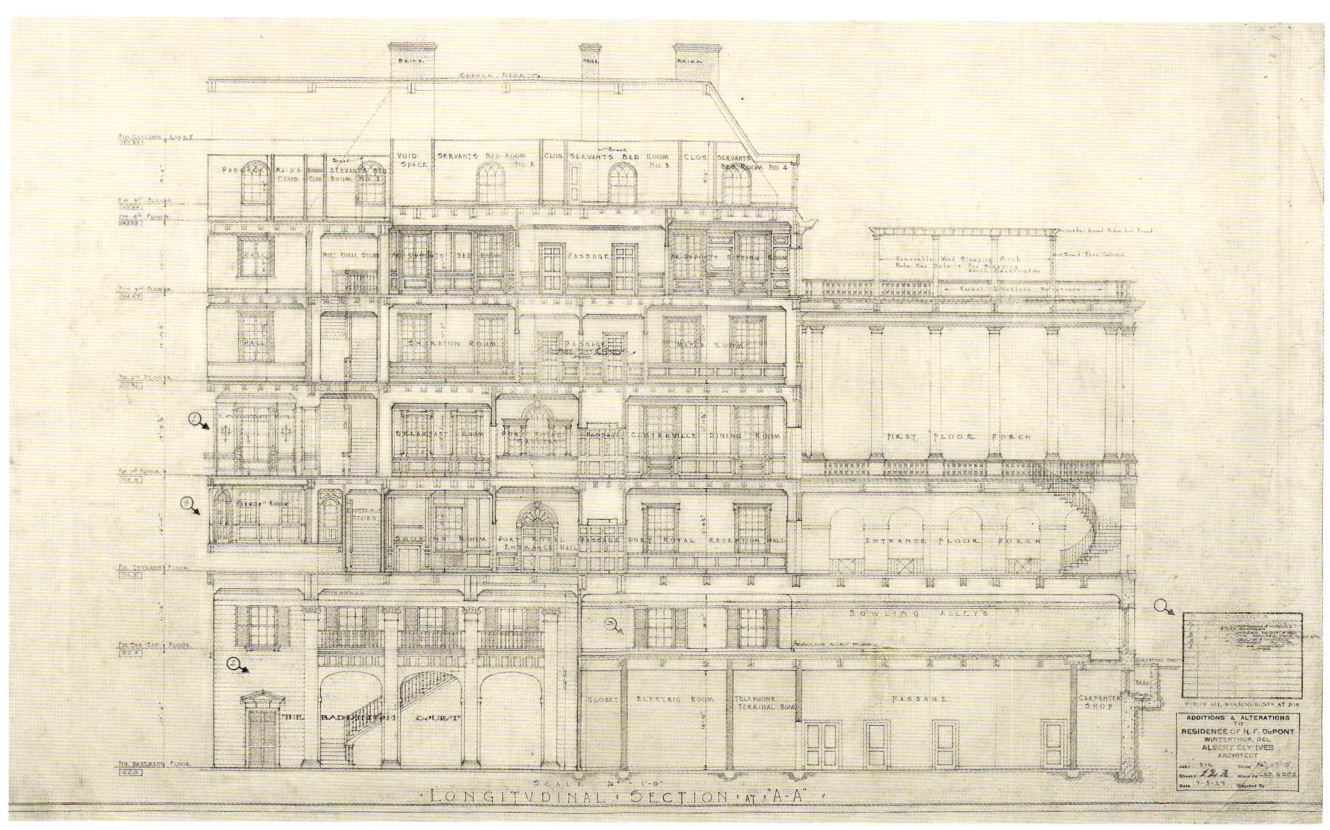

Albert Ely Ives, longitudinal section of the wing, ca. 1929

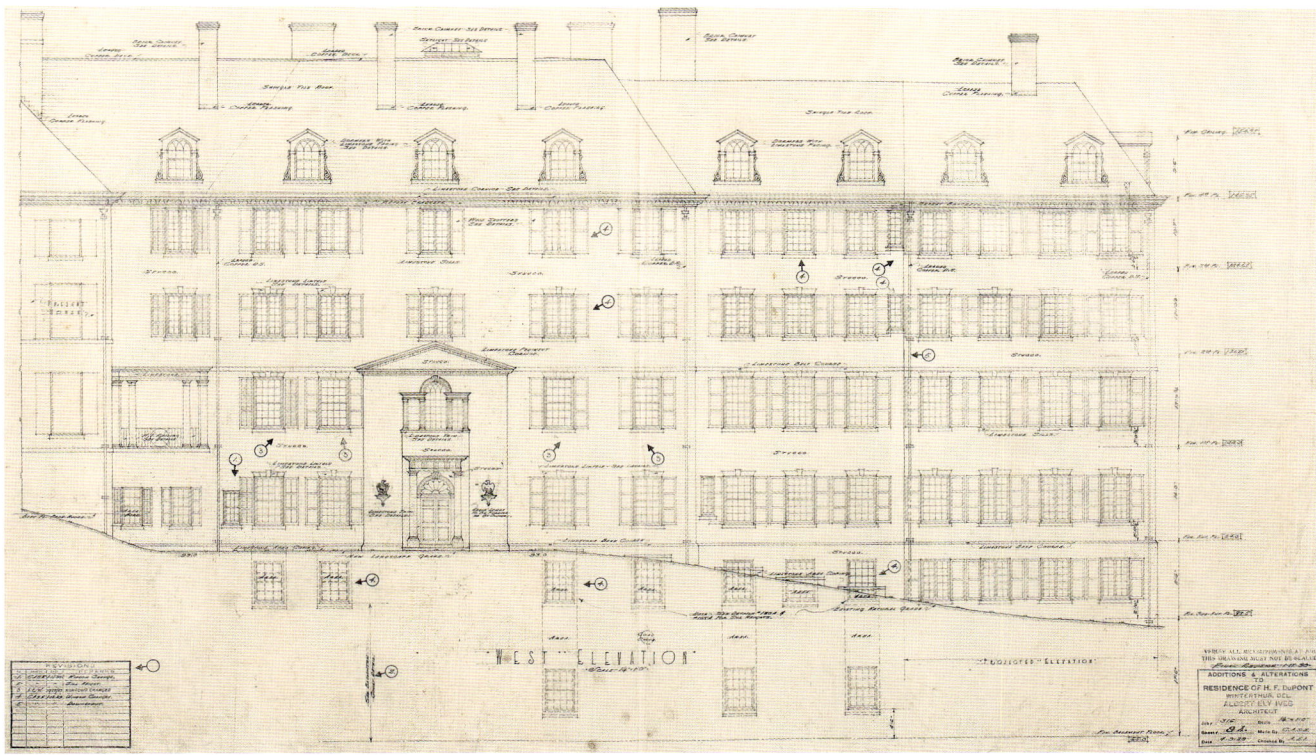

Albert Ely Ives, west elevation of the wing, ca. 1929

Aerial view, ca. 1935

ON THE FINAL DAY of 1926, 89-year-old Colonel Henry Algernon du Pont died, leaving his fortune and the country estate known as Winterthur to his 46-year-old only son. The Winterthur grounds encompassed more than 2,000 acres and included extensive gardens, 20 farms, 100 tenant houses, and a train station with a post office. Within a month of his father's death, Henry Francis, known as Harry, was "painting and doing over the floors in almost every room" of the 35-room French Renaissance–style house he inherited. Repainting the rooms was a temporary measure, as Harry had far grander plans. He envisioned Winterthur as an assemblage of American decorative arts that would surpass the collections at the recently opened American Wing of the Metropolitan Museum of Art in New York. Even before his father's death, he had begun to acquire antique paneled rooms for Winterthur, storing them in barns on the estate. By September 1928 he created a team to help realize his goal: landscape architect Marian Cruger Coffin, whom he knew from childhood; architect Albert Ely Ives, a recent Delaware transplant from the Addison Mizner firm in Palm Beach; and Massachusetts-based interior designer Henry Davis Sleeper. Charles O. Cornelius, an architect formerly with the American Wing at the Met, would supervise the installation of the historic interior architecture, which was carried out by Schleich Studios of New York. When Harry's cousin Anna Butler heard about the plans to change Winterthur into an American showplace, she was horrified: "Harry is going to fill Winterthur with wooden bowls full of apples!"[1]

Not everyone shared her view. John R. Schoemer, an antique hardware expert with the firm of Ostrander and Eshleman, was brought in as a consultant to the project. He met the team in Harry's New York apartment:

The servants' quarters had been cleared of all furniture and innumerable drafting tables set up. They were covered with a great variety of . . . the most amazing assembly of antique hardware I had ever seen. Mr. du Pont led the group from table to table, explaining the history of a few

South side of the house, ca. 1932

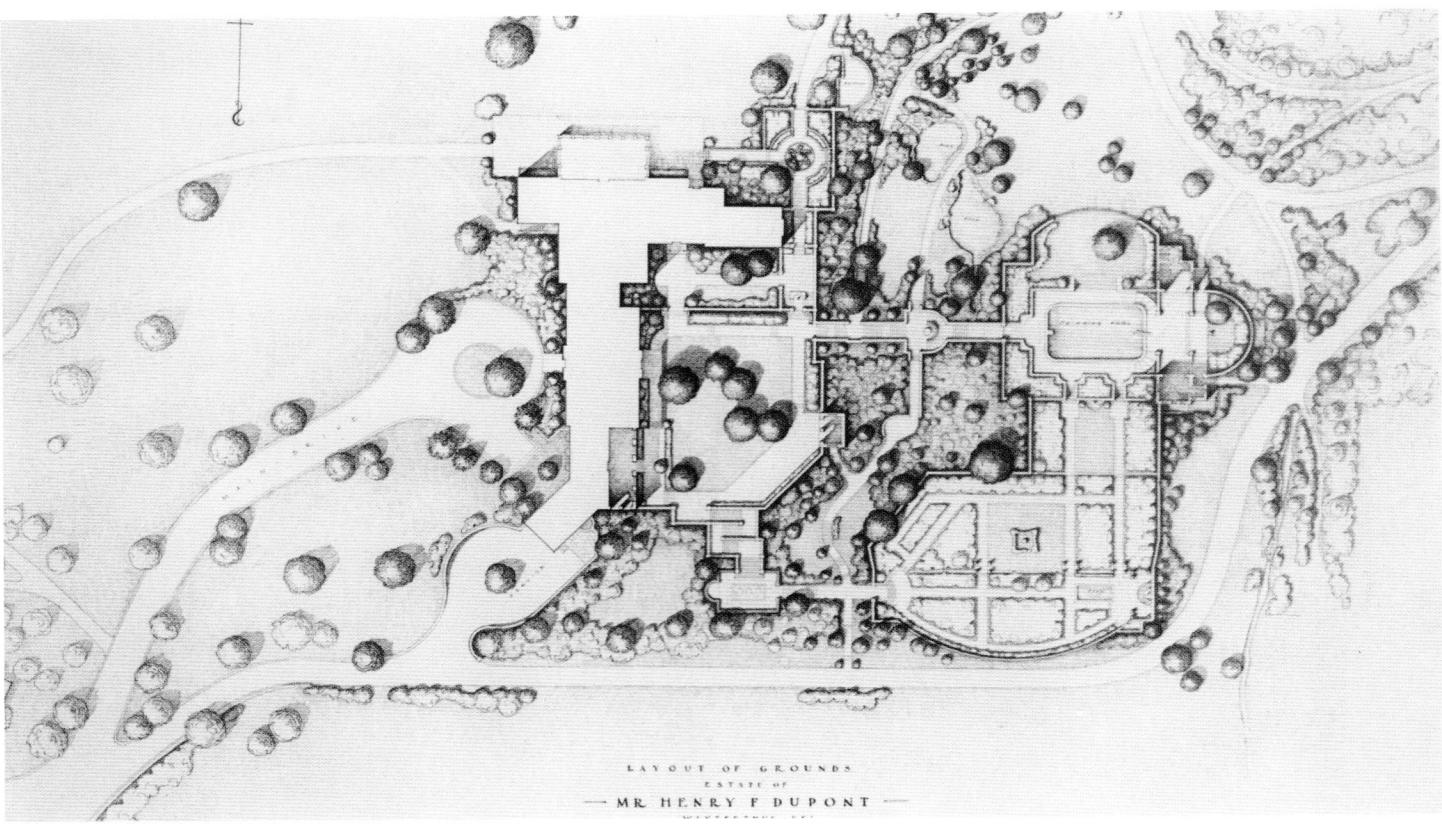

Marian Coffin's plan for the garden and grounds, ca. 1930

pieces, and telling us that this was only a small part of the collection. To familiarize me with the project, huge rolls of elevations, plans and details of the largest house I had ever seen were spread out before me. Large residential work was no novelty to anyone connected with Ostrander and Eshleman as the files continually contained orders from the Rockefellers, Vanderbilts, Astors, Goulds, Fords and a host of other fabulous American families; but viewing the plans of Winterthur was a new experience. Here was a building, which eventually was to be a house of 185 rooms, the majority with paneling, furniture, rugs, and hardware, all priceless antiques.[2]

Ground was broken July 1, 1929. A long, narrow wing, seven stories high, made of steel and concrete was added onto the south end of the remodeled house. Weekly photographs recorded every aspect of the construction site for a year. A temporary two-story office building was erected for the architectural and contracting staffs, and assorted storage sheds for building materials surrounded the site. The October stock market crash was ignored. Work continued unabated on the unified development of the house and grounds, with a Beaux Arts–style garden by Coffin that included one of the first heated swimming pools in America and an enormous iris garden. There was also a new 10-hole golf course, a children's play area with a jungle gym, swings, and a sandbox as well as a croquet and tennis court. This was all in addition to the preexisting estate Harry inherited, which included a William Robinson-style Wild Garden, a pinetum, and farms. Harry even oversaw construction work on the great barn at Winterthur's dairy (one of the finest Holstein breeding operations in the country), which burned to the ground in August 1930.

The house construction was a complicated affair and diverted Harry's attention from almost everything else. Ives's task was to build a wing of historical American style and blend it with the original house. He retained the roof line, casement windows, and stucco finish and applied these features to the new wing. He pulled off the turn-of-the-century

Box scroll garden, ca. 1931

French Renaissance detailing and switched the entrance facade from the north side to the west. The new wing was basically a streamlined box, with the new entrance a Jazz-Age riff on a 1762 Philadelphia country house called Port Royal. Ives enlarged the proportions of the door, smoothed out the architectural features, and applied an idealized cast stone version of the 18th-century house around the new front door to Winterthur. A sense of enclosure was created by angling the house—with the old house as the top cross bar and a service wing at a dogleg on the end. The house was decidedly undomestic in scale, but because of the surrounding trees and the way it was positioned in the hillside, there was a sense of horizontality rather than height, not unlike Mizner's 1926 Boca Raton Resort Hotel. The past was referenced, but the whole was resolutely modern.

Inside, the building was a labyrinth of display rooms, family living spaces, and sport and service areas. The reception rooms, halls, dining room, and the 11 bedrooms suites, each with bath and dressing room, were decked out in period architecture and furnishings. A bowling alley, Ping-Pong room, movie theater–badminton court, billiard room, and squash court provided entertainment for those uninterested in the antiques, although all the rooms, except for the service areas, were historicized in some degree. The golf locker room was decorated with du Pont's extensive collection of Near Eastern costumes, and the badminton court was filled with antique American eagles, urns, and furniture. A bronze windowed conservatory served as a transition space into the garden. The service areas were extensive, with two flower arranging rooms, a silver cleaning room, a shoe cleaning room, and designated storage rooms for everything from bedspreads to silver to electric light bulbs to wine. The laundry area included a large drying room with gas-heated floor racks and drying trays. The kitchen included a cooled pastry room as well as a walk-in refrigerator. There were two family elevators, plus a trunk lift and a dumbwaiter.

Harry, his wife, Ruth, and their two daughters moved back into the greatly enlarged house on April 1, 1931. That spring

WINTERTHUR

Stereoview, enclosed porch, 1935

Stereoview, south room, 1935

WINTERTHUR

Stereoview, entrance hall, 1935

Stereoview, sitting room, 1935

Staircase leading to the swimming pool, ca. 1931

Heating control room for the swimming pool, ca. 1935

Henry Francis du Pont and his sister, Louise du Pont Crowninshield

was spent hosting a cycle of house parties: 113 guests spent the night between April 24 and June 26. It was an ephemeral moment. When the family returned to Winterthur from the summer in Southampton, money troubles began. Superficial at first, Ruth wrote to her mother at the end of September, "I am going to cut down in every possible way, no more caviar, "terrap" or "pate." More serious efforts at economizing followed just a few weeks later, when they began laying off house, garden, and farm staff. A 1936 world cruise, which may have been taken for financial reasons, allowed the family to shutter the house for five months. In 1938 there were more layoffs and the guest bedroom floor was closed. Schoemer recalled the end of his project at Winterthur:

> The Great Depression was now forming to run its horrible, dreary course of almost a decade and little did we realize what lay ahead for us. I then thought Winterthur was only a link in the chain of future great houses to be built by America's financial giants. I often wonder what my reaction would have been in 1931 had I suspected Winterthur was destined to be the last; that other palatial estates would be selling at a fraction of their cost in the near future.[3]

Harry did manage to save the house and his collection by opening it to the public as a museum in 1951. His original plan, articulated in 1930, included detailed instructions about how the house would function as a museum after his death. That timeframe, however, had to be accelerated. After 1951 Harry and Ruth continued to live on the estate in a smaller house. They kept up the farms and garden and used the golf course and swimming pool until their deaths, hers in 1967, his in 1969.

The 1,000 remaining acres of Winterthur are now under conservation easement, ensuring that the landscape will not be changed. The naturalistic garden, extensive grounds, and museum are all open to visitors year-round.

GARDEN CLUB OF AMERICA TOUR
1929

Rare Images of du Pont Gardens

Performance in the Sundial Garden at Longwood, ca. 1926

The fountains at Longwood, ca. 1926

LAVISH GARDENS have graced du Pont houses since the family arrived in America in 1800. Before emigrating from France, E. I. du Pont took botany and horticulture classes in Paris at the Jardin des Plantes, which was founded in 1626 as a royal garden of medicinal plants. On his passport he declared himself a botanist. Once he and his family settled in Delaware, he turned his attention to the grounds of Eleutherian Mills. In an 1803 letter he wrote, "You are aware, my friend that being without a garden was the greatest deprivation; and it is the first thing that occupied my time."[1] He planted trees and shrubs and, over time, created a two-acre parterre garden of fruits, flowers, herbs, and vegetables. While his three sons were occupied with business and agriculture, his four daughters became avid horticulturists. They, in turn, encouraged their nieces and nephews. By 1900 every du Pont estate had a garden with greenhouses, and rare plants were passed along carefully to the next generation.

The great public gardens for which the Wilmington area is known today—Winterthur, Longwood, Mt. Cuba, Nemours, Gibraltar, and Goodstay—were thriving private residences before World War II. In 1918 the newly formed Garden Club of Wilmington provided an organized semi-public outlet for garden tours, talks, and competitions. Eight of the original 20 members were du Ponts. Even by Garden Club of America standards, the Garden Club of Wilmington was an exceptionally well-heeled group. In one set of meeting minutes, kudos were showered on a hostess who had remembered to provide lunch for the chauffeurs. Despite, or even perhaps because of, the drivers getting them to meetings, the gardeners working the soil, and the landscape architects creating the designs, the Garden Club of

Wilmington was a nexus of serious horticultural exchange. After the club was accepted into the Garden Club of America in 1920, the national organization was alerted to the wealth of extraordinary gardens around the Brandywine. In 1924 Charles Sprague Sargent, director of Harvard's Arnold Arboretum, wrote in the magazine *Horticulture* that the du Ponts were "a family which in the last four generations has made the neighborhood of Wilmington, Delaware, one of the chief centers of horticulture in the United States." Two years later, the Massachusetts Horticultural Society awarded Pierre du Pont the George Robert White medal, then the highest gardening honor in America. In a long feature on Pierre's Longwood and the award, *The New York Times* noted, "No single individual has done so much . . . to foster a love of flowers in this country." Other family members were being recognized nationally as well. The Horticultural Society of New York made H. F. du Pont an honorary vice president in 1928, the same year Ethel Hallock du Pont was elected vice president of the American Orchid Society.

Not coincidentally, the number of tourists to the Brandywine Valley swelled in concert with the du Ponts' renown for gardening excellence. On May 16, 1929, more than 1,000 members of the Garden Club of America visited a dozen Wilmington gardens, nine of which were owned by members of the du Pont family. The Garden Club Bulletin reported that the visitors "reveled in a horticultural dream" on viewing H. F. du Pont's sunken perennial garden at Winterthur; the peonies and orchids at Ethel Hallock du Pont's Stillpond; and the 60-foot water lily canal at Paulina du Pont Dean's Nemours, which was published in the August issue of *Country Life* that year. More obscure delights such as the water garden at Mary Chichester du Pont's Elton; the roses at Louisa du Pont Copeland's terraced garden; and the geometric, Marian Coffin-designed layouts at Lammot du Pont's St. Amour and his sister Bella's Gibraltar dazzled the group. The day visit concluded at Longwood with a dance performance and extraordinary fountain show. Rows of cots were provided for those too exhausted to stand. These photographs of Wilmington-area gardens were taken for the Garden Club of America in the 1920s and early 1930s.

The gardens at Longwood, ca. 1922

Longwood, ca. 1926 (top), ca. 1922 (bottom)

Marian Coffin-designed swimming pool at Gibraltar, 1922 (top); Garden at Elton, 1922 (bottom)

Marian Coffin-designed Boxwood Garden at Saint Amour, 1924

The Sundial Garden at Saint Amour, 1924 (top); The Sundial Garden at Winterthur, 1924 (bottom)

Clematis-covered gazebo in the Sunken Garden at Winterthur, 1923

APPLECROSS

ca. 1750, renovated 1929–31, ca. 1949

Residence of Donald and Wilhelmina du Pont Ross

The garden, 1985

Front facade, with the new addition to the right, 1931

IN THE LATE 19TH CENTURY, the Peter Gregg Farm, which had been in the Gregg family since 1732, was passed along in the du Pont family, from Henry to his son William, who sold it to the DuPont Company when he left town after his 1892 divorce. In 1923 William's older brother Henry Algernon bought the farm from the company, and in 1926 his son Henry Francis inherited it. A year later Henry Francis sold it so that it could be given as a wedding gift to Wilhelmina ("Mina") du Pont and her husband Donald Peabody Ross. The property—84 acres along a heavily traveled road close to the old DuPont Company mills—came with a stone house and barn. During the Colonial Revival rage of the late 1920s, both buildings were ripe for restoration. Jim Thompson, the apparent architect of the 1929–31 renovation, doubled the size of the house but kept the restraint and simplicity of the original.[1] An antique water pump accented the back door, one of the rare flights of Colonial Revival fancy on the house. The new addition was built on the side of the house farthest from the road, toward the barn. The views were of uninterrupted pasture, as clean-edged and unspoiled as the lines of the house.

To connect the house to the garden, which was located between the house and barn, an octagonal flagstone terrace was built. The lowest level of the 19th-century bank barn continued to be used for livestock (the Rosses kept a few cows and horses as well as chickens and a pig or two). The upper level of the barn, at a right angle to the house, was made into a picturesque centerpiece of the garden.

New York landscape architect Noel Chamberlin, who also worked for Mina's sister Paulina, designed the grounds of Applecross. He created a circular front drive and a series of garden terraces that could be entered from the driveway through an acorn-finial gate. The first level led to a fountain bordered on one side by the barn and the other by the octagonal flagstone terrace. Stone steps descended to the next terrace, which consisted of tightly structured flower beds and a summerhouse overlooking the pasture. An early feature of the garden was a grape arbor. Later in life, Mina explained,

The springhouse and farm gates, 1931

"My grandmother [Mary Belin du Pont] had one and my mother [Ethel Hallock du Pont] had one and I believe you can't raise children without one!"[2] The Rosses raised two daughters and a son at Applecross.

In the late 1940s, the Rosses added to the house an aluminum and glass sunroom designed in a modernist style by Victorine and Samuel Homsey; it was an interesting juxtaposition with Thompson's Colonial Revival addition. The interiors were spare with white-painted brick walls and plenty of room for plants. Heat was piped to the main house from the garage—a multipurpose building that also contained the laundry. The main residence was staffed by a cook, nanny, upstairs maid, butler, houseman, and laundress.

After the death of Mina's mother in 1951, some of her famous plant collections (tree peonies, orchids, African violets) and her Lord & Burnham greenhouses were moved to Applecross. In 1953 the Rosses hired Marian Coffin to extend the garden to include the tree peony collection of more than 100 plants. Mina, as ardent and serious a gardener as her mother, made Applecross into one of the showplaces of Wilmington.[3] Upon her death in 2000, the property was sold and is now a housing development.

Sunroom addition, ca. 1949

Sunroom interior, ca. 1949

APPLECROSS

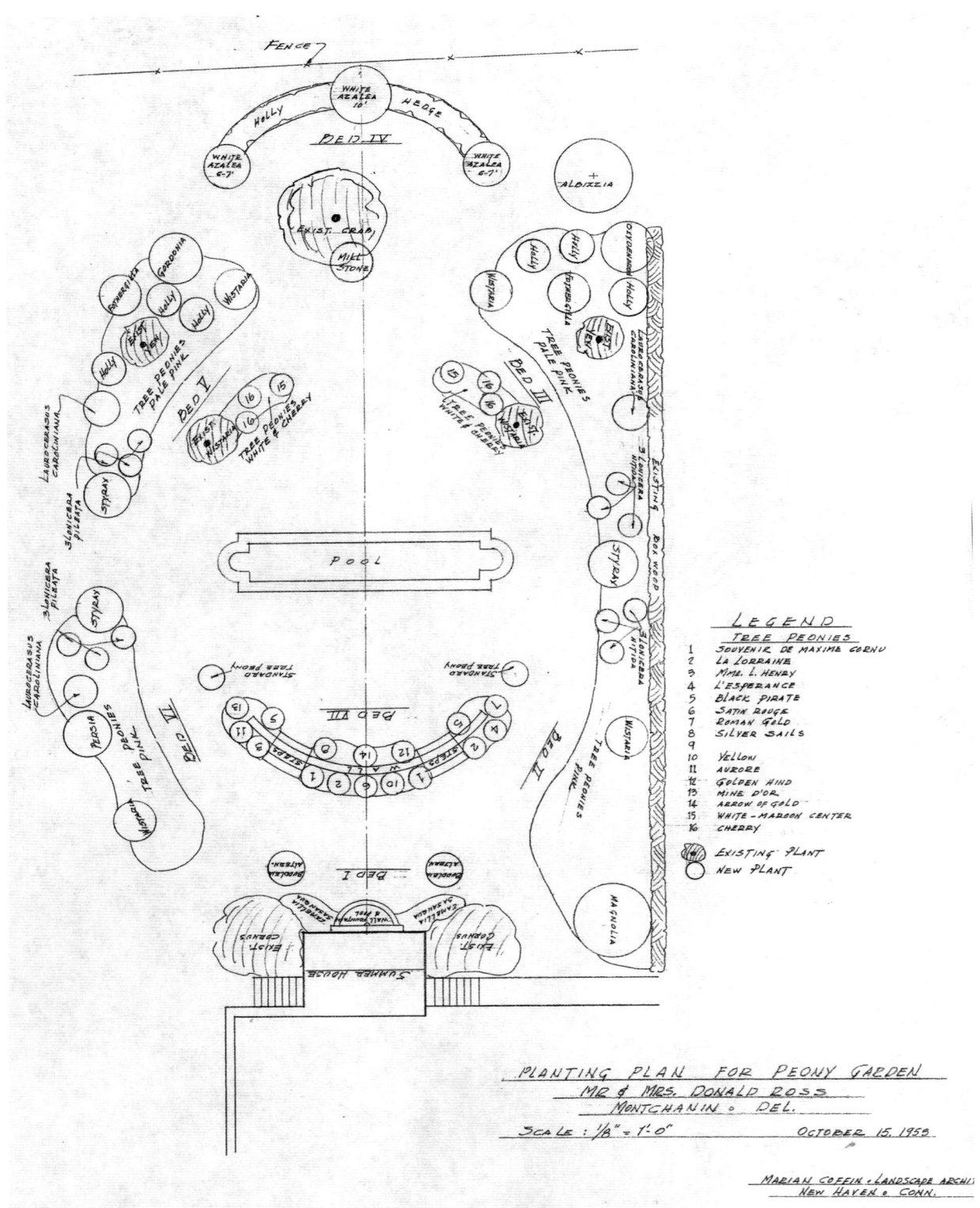

Marian Coffin garden plans, 1953

Mina Ross in the Homsey addition at Applecross, ca. 1949

MEOWN FARM

ca. 1930, renovated 1946

Residence of Isabella du Pont Sharp

The farm group at Meown, October 2008

Dovecote with Bella Sharp's house in the background, ca. 1932

Bella Sharp with doves at Meown

Meown, with the Homsey addition to the left, ca. 1950

NO BRANDYWINE FARM is more captivating than Isabella du Pont Sharp's Meown. Although Isabella, or Bella, as she was known, had little curiosity about design or architecture, her husband, Rodney, dedicated his life to these pursuits. The couple lived at Gibraltar on the outskirts of Wilmington. In the early 1930s, Rodney collaborated with architect Albert Ely Ives and builder A. L. Lauritsen on this 108-acre farm-retreat for Bella. It was a place where she could stable her horses, play bridge, and have tea with friends. It was a place all her own: hence, Meown.

A romantic combination of a Loire Valley–Brandywine farm, the centerpiece of Meown was an enormous stone barn with brick corbelling and a bell tower. There was an attached greenhouse for flowers, stalls for her horses, a detached dovecote, and a caretaker's cottage. Bella's house was not a home. It was simply one large room for entertaining, with a covered back porch overlooking the pasture, a tiny bathroom, and a kitchenette for drinks and sandwiches. Bella's son Bayard inherited Meown in 1946. "Bayard is desperate," H. F. du Pont, whose property Winterthur bordered Meown, wrote that year, "as he tried to fix Bella's Meown Farm for his house, and it cost him 200 percent more than it should have and he can't get it finished."

Just after World War II, Bayard's cousin, architect Victorine du Pont, and her husband, Samuel Homsey, helped Bayard renovate the house. A simple clapboard addition was constructed at a right angle to the stone core, a traditional Brandywine combination. A small service wing was extended off the other side. The interior spaces were less traditional. The Homseys created a series of modernist rooms with lots of built-in features. The master bedroom headboard hid a pivoting night table. The bathrooms had heated cabinets for drying towels and chic gray glass wash basins. The living room had polished brick floors and floor-to-ceiling windows. The contemporary style must have helped take the edge off the rather stifling quaintness of the surrounding farm buildings. Meown, which retains the name, is still owned and lived in by the family. Locals know it for the distinctive Galloway cattle that graze the land.

The living room, ca. 1950

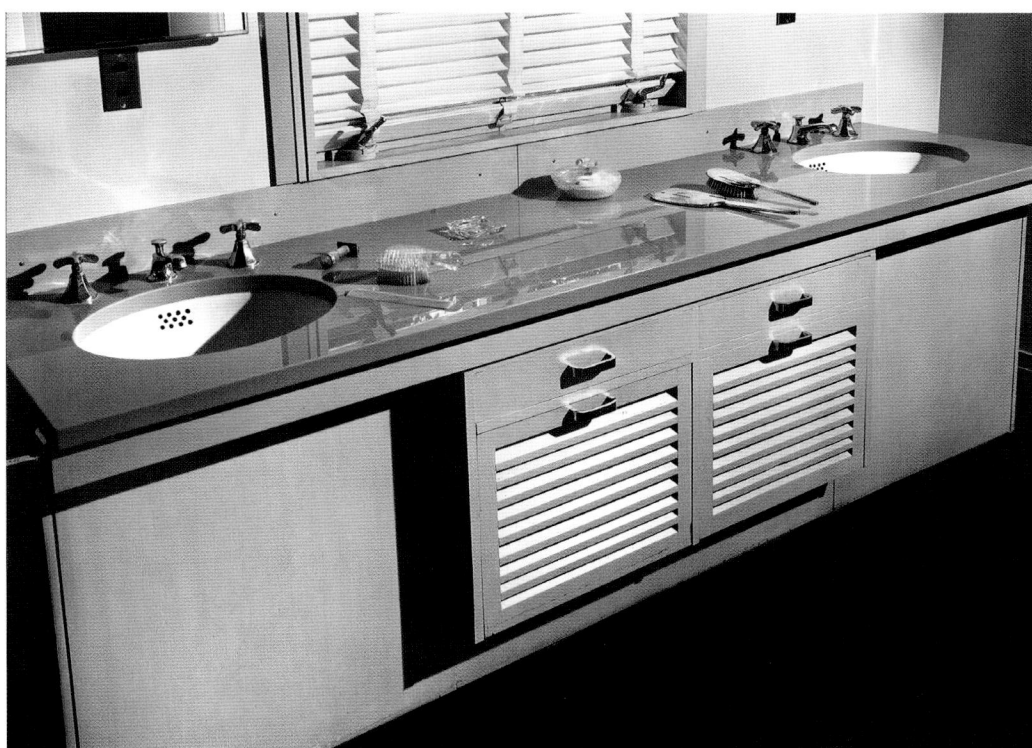

Renovated bathroom, ca. 1950

FAIR HILL

1930

Residence of E. Frances du Pont Morgan Rust

Fair Hill, ca. 1935

Entrance, ca. 1935

Entrance hall, ca. 1935

R. BROGNARD OKIE was the architect of choice among du Pont newlyweds in the late 1920s and 1930s. Okie's farmhouses suited the Gatsby generation's taste for breezy informality. The brown fieldstone and white clapboard exteriors—local materials used in traditional American ways—offered a stylish contrast to the castellated structures beloved by the older generation.[1] Okie, a popular architect on the Philadelphia Main Line, practiced independently. By the 1930s, he had developed a specialty restoring and reconstructing Pennsylvania landmarks such as the Betsy Ross house in Philadelphia and Pennsbury, the 18th-century William Penn estate. Okie houses of the 1920s and 1930s were more self-consciously period than earlier du Pont family Colonial Revival residences such as Granogue, Lyndham, and Longwood, with interiors consistent with the exterior architecture.

Okie's first three du Pont commissions were the result of a flurry of marriages among a group of school friends. Each couple received an Okie house in Wilmington, Delaware, as a wedding present. The first was in 1926 for Elizabeth Wrenn's marriage to S. Hallock du Pont, Pierre du Pont's nephew. Elizabeth, from Washington, D.C., was a friend of Pierre's niece Esther, who had attended Holton Arms, the girls' preparatory school in Washington. Esther's father, Lammot du Pont, funded the second Okie commission—the remodeling of an old farmhouse called the White Farmhouse in preparation for Esther's September 1928 wedding to Campbell Weir.[2] Esther's cousin, Frances du Pont, another Holton Arms classmate,

Dining room, ca. 1950

received the third Okie house after her 1927 elopement with pilot Richard Morgan. This last house, called Fair Hill, was completed in 1930.

Okie built three other houses for du Ponts in the 1930s. Between 1930 and 1932, he created an addition for Buena Vista, an 1847 house recently inherited by 40-year-old Alice du Pont and her husband of 10 years, C. Douglass Buck, then governor of the state. In 1935 Okie constructed a stone, Georgian block-style house on the Red Clay Creek for Margaret Wilson Lewis and her husband, Henry Belin du Pont, another of Pierre's nephews. The last house Okie built for a du Pont was Ridgely, constructed in 1940 for the young Nicholas du Pont, who had grown up at Owl's Nest.

Frances du Pont Morgan's Fair Hill (built 1929–30) is the best documented of the du Pont-Okie houses, with more than 300 architectural drawings in the Okie papers at the Pennsylvania State Archives, as well as an extensive collection of photographs and correspondence in the archives and with the family. Fair Hill displays all the quintessential Okie characteristics: steel and concrete framing clad in clapboard and fieldstone; cypress-shingle roof with large stone chimneys; and a high level of craftsmanship. A wealth of regional architectural detail distinguishes the building: pent-roof entrances, segmental-arch window lintels, and box roof cornices. The windows were built into deep, curved plaster frames. Okie was unstinting with Colonial Revival fancies: lanterns on shelves decorate the entries; iron tulip hinges and thumb latches ornament the doors; and almost every room has a capacious fireplace filled with hooks and inset spaces for antique tools and cooking implements.

Fair Hill was spread over 200 acres. Okie designed the springhouse and garage with an upstairs apartment as well as the 40-room main residence with attached guest house. Frances du Pont's L-shaped abode was thoroughly up to date

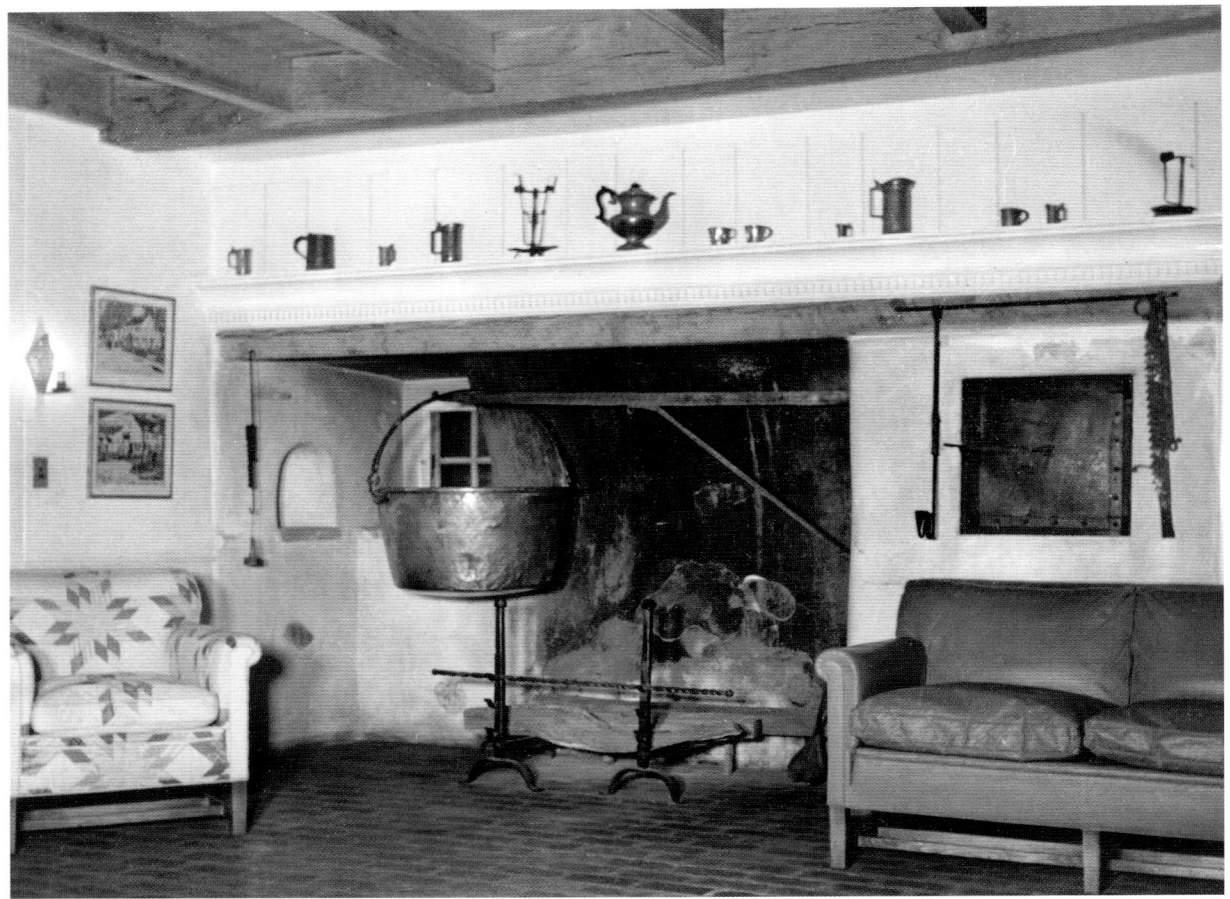
Tap room, ca. 1935

Library fireplace, ca. 1935

Boxwood and rose garden designed by Thomas Sears, ca. 1935

but, just as the fieldstone and clapboard hid the concrete and steel, historical style in the rooms sheathed the modern conveniences. Tin candle sconces held electric bulbs. A hunting-print cover disguised the telephone book in the pine-paneled library. Richard Morgan's flying trophies vied with the polished antique copper and brass on the library fireplace mantel. Cocktail parties were held in the basement tap room, with its ceiling of exposed old beams and floor of antique bricks. The 11 bathrooms combined antique mirrors with chromium-plated fixtures and crystal towel bars.

The historic theme continued even in the carefully planned storage and service rooms. The flower arranging room had Revolutionary-era thumb latches on the door, and the broom closet between the kitchen and the servant's dining room featured reproduction iron hinges with hand-hammered nails.

Okie also seems to have been actively involved in furnishing the house. Bills for Fair Hill from antiques dealers funneled through his office. The house was sprinkled with corner cupboards, hooked rugs, and hunting prints. It was decorated in what advice books of the period called the Simple Style: plain walls, ruffled curtains, spareness of bibelots.

Okie-designed pump house, ca. 1950

Most of the existing correspondence about the house concerns the hardware, which Okie carefully chose. As was typical in the 1920s, the hardware was picked out in black against the white walls, doors, and windows. Dr. Charles Berwind Montgomery, the leading authority on Schuylkill Valley history at the time, was brought in as a consultant. He purchased Pennsylvania German wrought iron for Fair Hill and wrote a 10-page description of each item. Not all the hardware was used as originally intended. The top hinges on the built-in shell-back china cupboard in the dining room were pried off a Conestoga wagon box and straightened out for the door. Myron Teller, a highly regarded Hudson Valley architect and metalsmith, reproduced matching hinges for the lower part of the door. Teller and Montgomery also provided antique and reproduction hardware to Essie du Pont Weir at the White Farmhouse and Alice du Pont Buck at Buena Vista while they were working on Fair Hill. Okie had to sort out the confusion about which du Pont got what hardware.

Thomas Sears, a landscape designer with a specialty in Colonial Revival gardens, designed the garden at Fair Hill, setting the house within a complex of boxwood paths and boxwood-lined terraces. There was a rose garden, and iris,

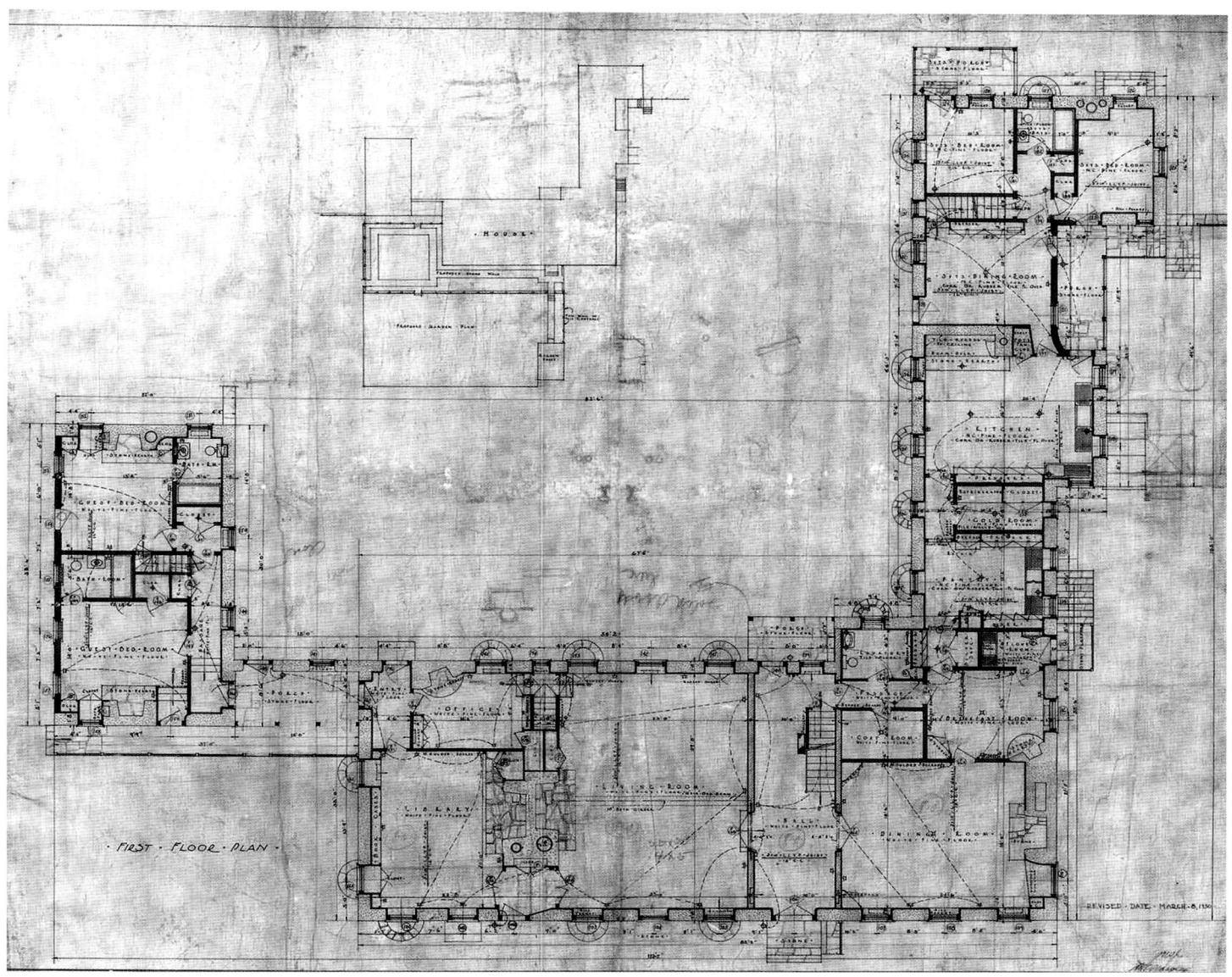

First floor plan, October 11, 1929

tulips, and lilies bloomed in the spring. Unlike most of her relatives, Frances du Pont was not particularly interested in horticulture, although she liked flower arranging.

Frances lived at Fair Hill (she and Morgan divorced and she later married Gordon Rust) until her death in 1975. Throughout the decades, she kept scrapbooks of the changes she made to the house. Wallpaper, upholstery, and paint samples fill the pages, each dated—a treasure trove of invaluable information about changing fashions. Fair Hill has been sold and remodeled several times since 1975, and it continues today as a contemporary example of the Colonial Revival. The other five houses Okie built for du Ponts also survive. Three are still in family hands and work well for modern families, providing evidence of Okie's success in designing enduring domestic architecture.

BELLEVUE

1855, renovated 1931–33

Residence of William du Pont Jr.

Aerial view of the garden and riding stables (upper left), July 27, 1940

Bellevue, the 1855 structure before renovation

WHEN WILLIAM DU PONT died in 1928, his daughter, Marion, inherited his main residence, Montpelier, the historic James Madison plantation that du Pont had purchased in 1900. His son, William du Pont Jr., came into Bellevue, an 1855 Gothic Revival castle set on more than 450 acres north of Wilmington.[1] Almost immediately, William morphed his legacy into a replica of Montpelier, where he and Marion had grown up.

William, who had achieved renown in the equestrian world as a breeder and racetrack designer, tended to shun architects. Bellevue was the second Montpelier replica he built. He and his first wife, Jean Austin, had re-created the Madison house at Foxcatcher, the large, Pennsylvania Austin family farm where they raised their four children. In 1931, assisted by contractor John A. Bader and engineer Bernard T. Converse, William likewise remodeled Bellevue. He built over the existing structure, and the floor plan of the house was more reflective of the 1855 building than Montpelier. The exterior, however, with its yellow painted stucco finish and pillared garden facade, was as close as possible to that of his childhood home. Most of the outbuildings at Bellevue were purely functional structures, purchased by mail order (as his father had done at Montpelier and at Bellevue) or older farm buildings remodeled to suit the new purpose. Exceptions to this rule were the playhouse next to the swimming pool, which was designed to resemble the Montpelier house, and the handsome twin gatehouses designed by Massena & du Pont in 1933.[2]

Bellevue, 1930s

Willie, as William Jr. was called, was less interested in horticulture than the rest of the family. Bellevue's horseshoe-shape walled garden was filled with dwarf boxwood cut to look like equestrian accessories. Flowers and winter vegetables were grown in two large greenhouses and a smaller growing house.

Sport was the purpose of Bellevue. The 482-square-foot trophy room was more than twice the size of the drawing room, and an underground tunnel led from the nine-bedroom house to the nearby sports complex. Inside was a bowling alley, badminton and squash courts, swimming pool, and a tennis court.[3] A five-furlong horse track dominated the landscape. The equestrian center included two indoor tracks, a hunter barn, a race barn, an enormous dumbbell-shape riding school, and a seven-bedroom jockey house. There was also an outdoor tennis court and swimming pool. The playhouse contained a kitchen and living room as well as changing rooms. The estate had dairy, steer, and poultry farms and, in the best Virginia tradition, a ham house. Estate staff lived in the boardinghouse or in one of 14 tenant houses. Also on the premises were a train station, post office, and three gatehouses.

William divorced Jean Austin in 1940. As part of her settlement, she inherited Foxcatcher Farm. In 1947 Willie married

BELLEVUE

William du Pont Jr. and his sister Marion at Montpelier, March 1902

tennis star Margaret Osborne, whose six grand-slam singles titles included three U.S. championships. Bellevue was only a small part of Willie's vast real estate holdings, which included Fairhill, a 7,000-acre estate that straddled the Maryland-Pennsylvania border.

The state of Delaware purchased the Bellevue estate in 1976. Today it is open to the public as a park, and the main residence serves as a conference center and wedding facility.

HOD HOUSE

1931

Residence of Crawford and Margaretta du Pont Greenewalt

Aerial view, with Dripping Spigots under construction in the background, 1939

Terrace with dining room door to the left and library door to the right, ca. 1935

IN 1931 MARGARETTA DU PONT and her husband of five years, Crawford H. Greenewalt, built a portable Hodgson House on 550 acres outside Wilmington. Founded in the early 1890s, the E. F. Hodgson Company of Massachusetts was one of the first prefabricated housing factories in America. Ernest Franklin Hodgson developed what he called the Hodgson System—wooden modular parts locked in place with a wedge keybolt. The cedar house frame was covered in redwood clapboard and roofed in redwood shingles. Hodgson Houses came in an array of sizes and purposes: dog kennels and children's playhouses, garages and bungalows, oversize army barracks, and hospital annexes. Advertisements in magazines such as *House & Garden* promised "a Cozy Cottage—Quickly." Edward J. Steichen, Mrs. Andrew Carnegie, and Marshall Field gave testimonials, and catalogs claimed that there were Hodgson Houses on "some of America's finest estates—Astor's, Ames's, Belmont's, Cabot's, Du Pont's."

The Greenewalts set what they called the Hod House high on a hill, with open views extending over the countryside. The Hodgson Company typically shipped the house components by train, and a house the size of the one purchased by the Greenewalts could have been assembled within two days. The Greenewalts arranged the parts into a modified H shape and placed them on 18-inch concrete blocks enclosed in a skirt of lattice. A bedroom wing and a service wing were connected by a living room and dining room that overlooked a brick terrace. The Greenewalts chose French doors for the rooms overlooking the terrace and paired casement windows throughout the house with crescent-ornamented shutters. The garage unit attached to the end of the bedroom wing made it longer than the service wing. The servants' bedrooms jutted out at a right angle from the service wing.

The house was a rural summer retreat for the couple and their children (born 1929, 1931, and 1937). They spent the rest of the year in town in an Albert Ely Ives–designed house on 11th Street. Every summer in the 1930s, the household (parents, children, cook, maid-waitress, nursemaid, and driver) packed up and stayed in the country as late into the

HOD HOUSE

Shooting practice, ca. 1935

The Greenewalts (center) and friends, ca. 1935

Hodgson playhouse at the Greenewalt property, ca. 1935

fall as possible. Life at the Hod House was an outdoor idyll that revolved around picnicking, shooting, swimming, riding, and deck tennis.

The interior of the house was exceptionally airy. Nearly every room had a cross-breeze. The only warmth came from a large fireplace in the living room and small electric heaters in the bathrooms. Tan-color beaverboard walls, soft enough to hold thumbtacks, lined the walls. The floorboards were narrow pine, and the furnishings were casual: wicker, iron, chintz. Overnight guests had the choice of a guest room in the bedroom wing or a sofa bed in the library.

An avid gardener, Margaretta lined the entrance drive with oaks and landscaped the grounds with flowering shrubs, shade trees, and conifers. Vines and roses climbed up the exterior walls of the house. A little Hod playhouse was set up next to a huge sandbox.

The Greenewalts' land included the Burrows Run stream, ponds, upland meadows, and woodland. A preexisting farm, Coverdale, which they named after the Wilmington street where they lived as newlyweds, was run by a farmer who lived in the old farmhouse. Once a week he met with Margaretta, who oversaw the property. They grazed steer and raised chickens, vegetables, wheat, corn, and barley, and there was even a brief experiment with sheep. The hillside below the house was planted in table grapes. There was no dairy, as the household milk came from Granogue, where Margaretta's parents lived.

Crawford, who later became president of the DuPont Company, was a chemist during the nine summers the family lived in the Hod House. In 1939 he was named director of the Experimental Station at the DuPont Company. That year he and Margaretta commissioned local architect William E. Martin

Construction of Dripping Spigots, 1939

to build a permanent house for their family on the property. Margaretta, who disliked the practice of naming houses, dubbed the new residence Dripping Spigots. Crawford's metalworking shop, which included a darkroom, occupied one end of the first floor of the sprawling Martin-designed stone house. After moving into Dripping Spigots, the Greenewalts sold the Hod House to a neighbor, who moved it in pieces by truck to nearby Centreville, Delaware, where it remains today.

In 1990 Crawford and Margaretta donated 110 acres of their land to the Delaware Nature Society. At Crawford's death in 1993, the remainder of the farm was left to the Old Kennett Foundation, a landholding entity managed by W. H. Frederick Jr. and the Greenewalt children. In 1997 the foundation gave 229 acres, including the Coverdale farm buildings, to the Delaware Nature Society for education and preservation. Dripping Spigots was sold along with 22 acres to provide an endowment.

MT. CUBA

1935–37

Residence of Lammot du Pont and Pamela Copeland

Entrance gates, 1937

Garden facade, 1937

EARLY IN THE SUMMER of 1935 Lammot du Pont Copeland and his wife, Pamela Cunningham of Connecticut, began looking for a site in Delaware for their first home. Lammot's mother, Louisa du Pont Copeland, had left him some land in the DuPont Company yards, right on the Brandywine River, but Pamela dismissed the spot as damp and viewless. Henry Francis du Pont suggested his Indian Springs Farm just north of the Winterthur estate. Too remote, said Lammot. Eugene du Pont had 126 acres of corn and wheat fields in a hilly area, and Mt. Cuba, as the 400-foot hill was called, reminded Pamela of her home state: "I fell in love with the property and had it not been that Mr. H. B. du Pont had just about completed building his house right next door to us, I don't think that Mr. Copeland would have ever left the Brandywine."[1]

Aficionados of American history and the decorative arts, the Copelands were beguiled by the recent renovations at Colonial Williamsburg and at H. F. du Pont's Winterthur, Lammot's cousin's house. H. F., who was particularly fond of Pamela, advised the couple to buy the antique interior woodwork before construction began; "otherwise," he warned, "it is hopeless and most expensive." Period paneling from five states was acquired and sent to Wilmington cabinetmaker American Car & Foundry. To design the house, the Copelands hired Lammot's cousin Victorine and her husband, Samuel Homsey. The Homseys had worked on Lower Louviers with Philadelphia builder J. S. Cornell & Son, and they chose to use the firm again for Mt. Cuba. John S. Cornell Jr. later wrote that the Copeland job helped keep his firm out of bankruptcy during the Great Depression.[2]

Colonial Revival was a stylistic departure for the Homseys, who went on to specialize in the International Style. The two met head-on in Mt. Cuba, a steel and concrete structure swathed in Williamsburg genuine handmade colonial brick. Photographs commissioned after Mt. Cuba was completed shows it as a stark Tidewater residence. The empty landscape, recently shorn of crops, emphasized the spare geometry of the Homseys' design.

The conservatory, ca. 1940

The house was built with modern living in mind: plenty of storage, an easy entertaining circuit, and intimate upstairs family rooms. The second floor had 10 full bathrooms; the first had a powder room and men's room. Conveniences included an elevator, an incinerator, and walk-in cold storage in the kitchen and basement. These 20th-century amenities were not hidden within the historic framework but allowed equal reign. Although Pamela wrote about the charm of old woodwork, there was nothing quaint about Mt. Cuba.

The first floor consisted of a wide center hall leading to a dining room on the left and a living room on the right. Both rooms were paneled in high-quality 18th-century American woodwork and filled with American antiques, primarily Chippendale. The wing on the living room side of the house led to the conservatory, library, and study. The wing on the dining room side was service: wine storage, silver vault, and two rooms for overnight kitchen staff. The upstairs central block featured family bedrooms. Guest rooms were on the conservatory side, and female staff rooms were over the kitchen. Among the storage and mechanical spaces, the basement had a shooting range for Lammot, a laboratory, a dog's bath, and a laundry.

In 1935 landscape architect Thomas Sears, in midcareer and already renowned for his Colonial Revival work, con-

Entrance hall, ca. 1940

Dinner party at Mt. Cuba, with Pamela Copeland (foreground), ca. 1950

Pamela Copeland's dressing room, ca. 1940

sulted on the integration of the house and garden. The long driveway began in a valley and wound up to the house. The drive cut through bedrock; when completed, the blasted areas looked raw, but a rock garden softened the look. In front of the house, Sears created a walled forecourt with a south-facing terrace garden behind it, an allée of sweet gum, an allée of lilac, a greenhouse area, and a capacious cutting garden.

Agriculture at Mt. Cuba was supplemented by that from Andelot, a large farm the Copelands owned in Kent County, Maryland.[3] World War II interrupted the landscaping work at Mt. Cuba, and the planned Olympic-size pool was never built. A tennis court was one of the first major outdoor projects undertaken after the war, and in 1949 Marian Coffin was hired to redevelop the formal garden areas. As entertaining expanded in the 1950s, more tenant houses were built on the estate, and the garden continued to expand. A pool complex was finally completed in 1958, and the greenhouse range was more fully developed as Pamela became a serious horticulturist.

Perhaps the most significant change occurred in 1965. Seth Kelsey was hired to design a native garden at Mt. Cuba, and the Copelands began to realize their dream of turning the estate into a botanical park. In the 1970s, a 19th-century iron garden house that had once graced Lammot's grandmother's garden at Old Nemours was prominently placed along one of the landscaped ponds. Today Mt. Cuba is open to the public as a nonprofit center for the study of Piedmont flora.

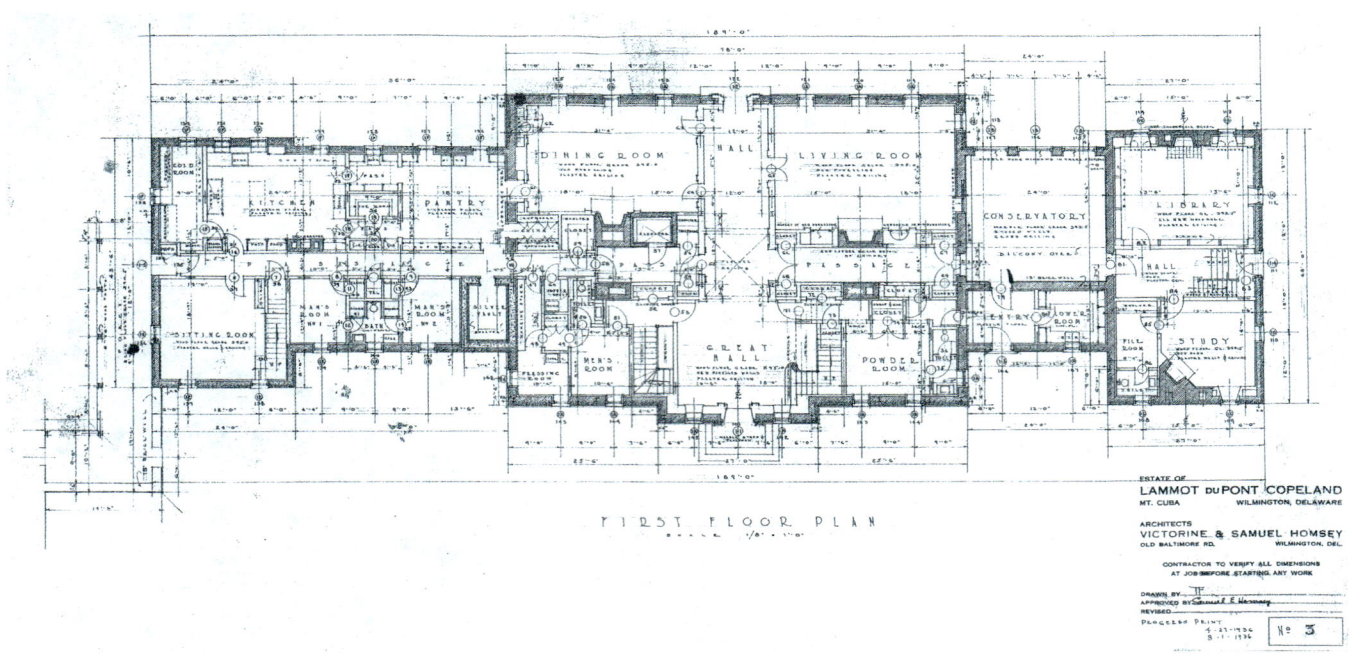

First floor plan, 1936

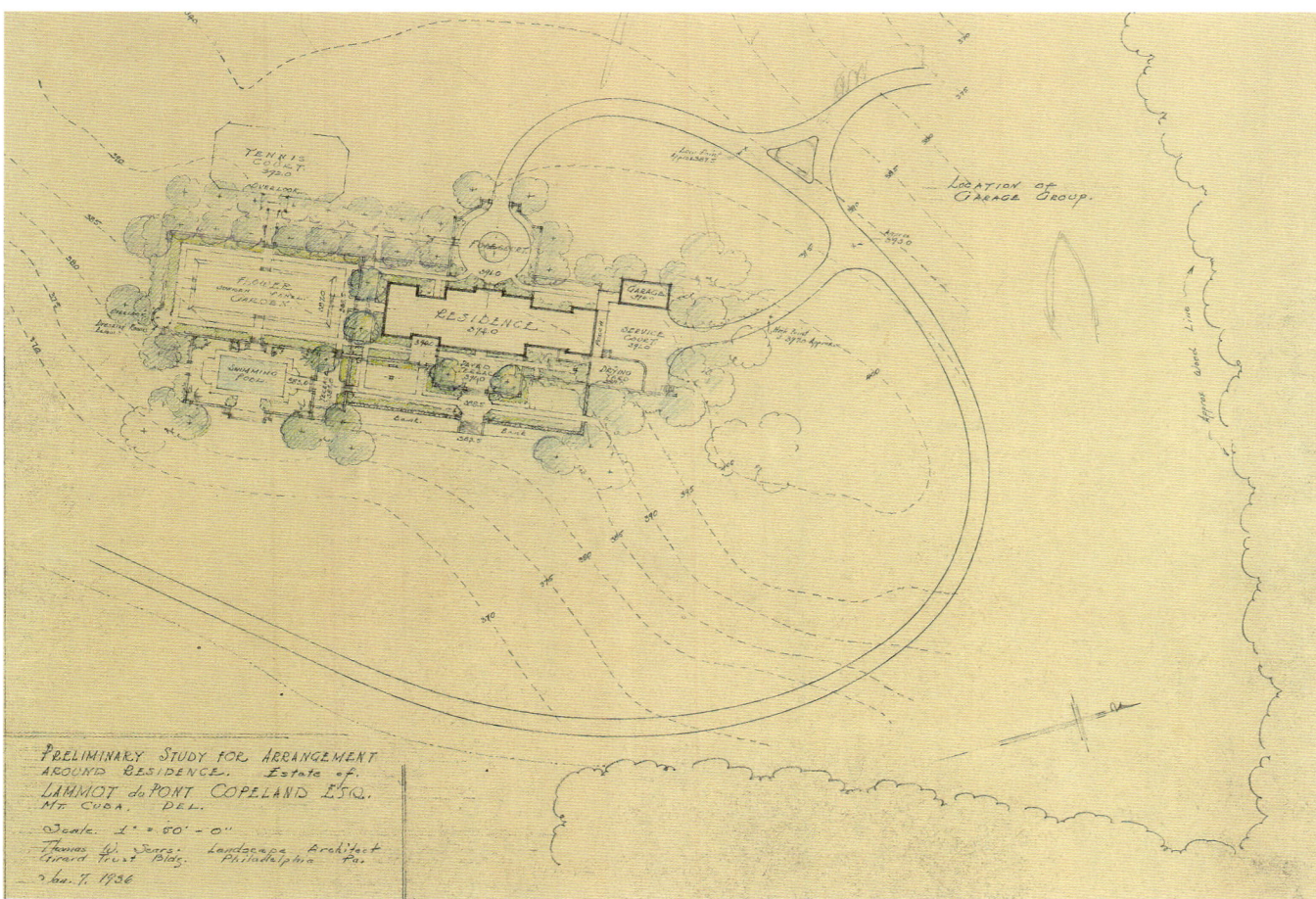

Thomas Sears garden plan, January 7, 1936

Iron garden house transplanted from Old Nemours

OBEROD

1935–37

Residence of Harry and Jane du Pont Lunger

Front facade, 1938

Gates, 1937

IN 1934 JANE DU PONT married Harry W. Lunger. One year later, she bought the first 108 of 165 acres for their planned estate from her cousin Lammot du Pont Jr. He charged her the nominal sum of $10. The Lungers named their estate Oberod after a poem written by Jane's late father, Philip du Pont: "We lived in the land of Oberod/ I and my wife and a little god/ And we were as happy as we could be."[1]

Ground was broken on November 26, 1935, and work was completed 18 months later. The Philadelphia firm of DeArmand, Ashmead & Bickley designed Oberod during the height of the Lindbergh baby kidnapping trial.[2] The Lungers reacted to the general climate of fear by installing an elaborate security system in the house. Campbell Teletector Company hooked up an "Interior Intrusion Detection System," and a control panel in the master bedroom worked the outdoor floodlights. The house, set deep in the property, could be reached only by passing through a pair of matching gatehouses.

Sitting in a former corn field, the U-shaped house was practically impenetrable; masonry construction was reinforced with steel webs, and the floors were concrete.[3] A gated cobblestone automobile forecourt lent the entrance a picturesque quality. The limestone-trimmed, whitewashed stone building was conceived in a kind of streamlined Norman style, and a three-story tower to the left of the front door broke up the geometry's monotony. Bernard Heatherley of Philadelphia supplied the ornamental metalwork, which included steel French garden doors. The hip roof was terra-cotta over gypsum slabs.

The house was arranged in a classic tripart, with the service wing opposite the intimate family areas. The connecting center wing held three large, linked entertaining spaces on the first floor: hall, dining room, and living room. The second floor contained a succession of children's rooms (the Lungers would eventually have five children). The basement featured a movie screening room, a billiard room, and Harry's woodworking shop. The machinery room—the steam heating system was fueled with propane gas, the cleanest fuel available—and mechanic's room were beneath the service wing.

Garden terrace, 1937

Steel-frame door to the garden terrace, 1937

Lewis & Valentine Company planting trees, 1937

Thomas Sears watercolor sketch of the proposed swimming pool, ca. 1937

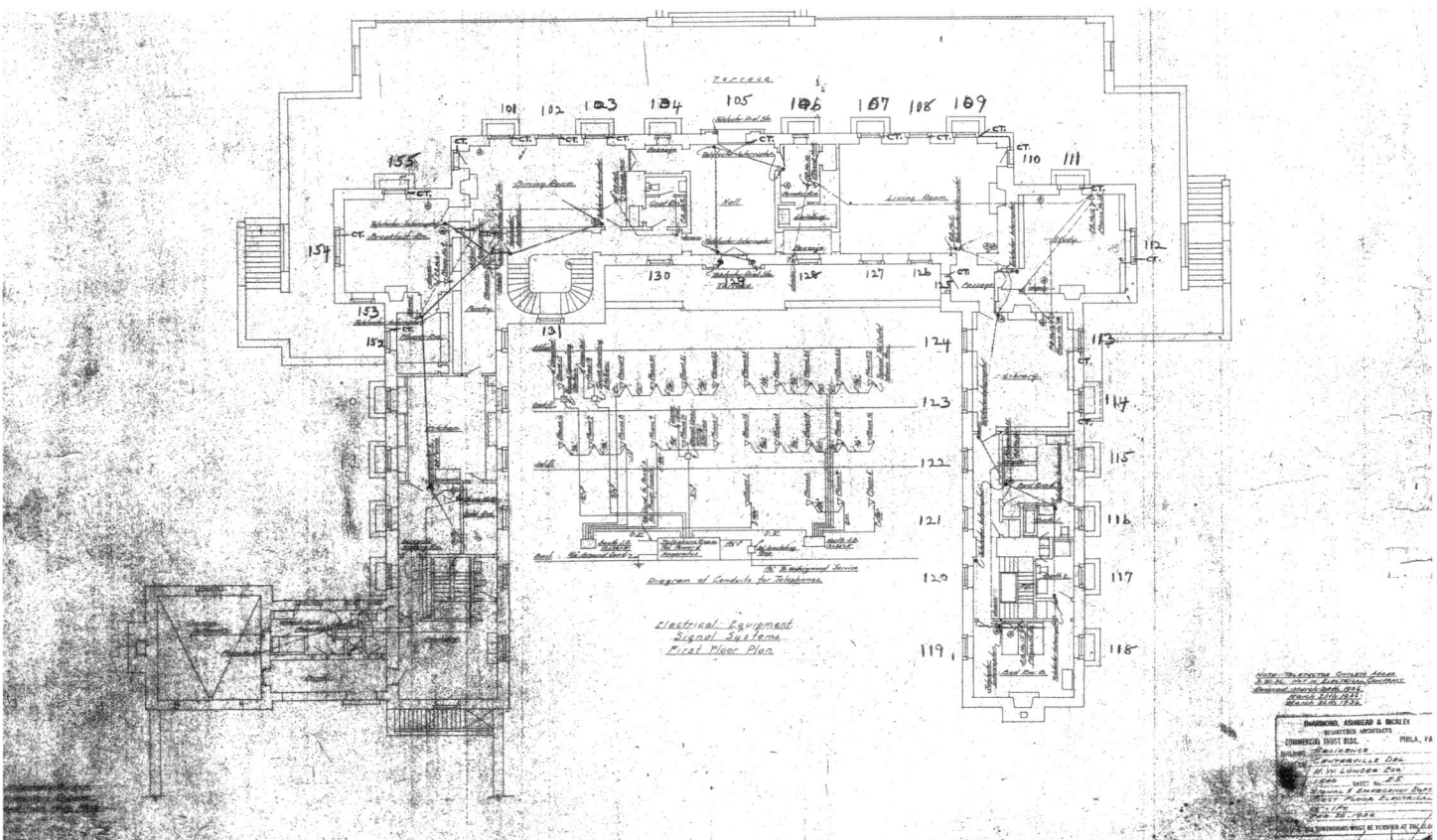

First floor plan, 1935

The watchman's room was next to the garage. The internal telephone system had 27 separate connections.

It was quite a house for a 21-year-old. Fair Hill, the estate of Jane's sister, was about a mile down the road. Designed by Brognard Okie, Fair Hill was Colonial Revival within and without. At Oberod Jane opted for more of a mix—a French Provincial exterior furnished with a mélange of antique French Provincial pieces, contemporary upholstered furniture, and American antiques.[4] Philadelphia interior designer Walter J. Johnson, who worked with art collector Henry P. McIlhenney among others, sold her a Federal-style dining room sideboard and hand-painted Chinese wallpaper. Not all rooms were historical. The second-floor sitting room had a chromium and glass fireplace surround and birch doors.

The house had no garden or greenhouse, which was unusual for a du Pont home. It did have a cutting and vegetable garden, which were practical necessities. During construction, the Lewis & Valentine firm brought in large trees to ornament the grounds. Thomas Sears, who had designed the garden at Fair Hill and the Copelands' garden at Mt. Cuba, drew a sketch for a swimming pool at Oberod, but it was never built.

After Harry died, in 1976, Jane gave the house with 40 acres to the Episcopal Church as a retreat. In 1980 she hired Homsey Architects to build a smaller house on the property for herself. In 2007 the main house and 40 acres were sold to a private buyer.

TULIP HOLLOW

1939–40

Residence of Samuel Eldon and Victorine du Pont Homsey

Front entrance, ca. 1940

TULIP HOLLOW

Living room/dining room at Tulip Hollow, divided by sliding walls. The painting above the fireplace, by Henriette Wyeth Hurd, is of Eldon du Pont Homsey, ca. 1940.

VICTORINE DU PONT met her future husband, Samuel Eldon Homsey, in his hometown of Boston, where they worked together at the architectural firm of Allen & Collens. During the Great Depression there were few architectural commissions so the couple traveled in Europe and Mexico; Samuel, an accomplished watercolorist, painted and exhibited. By 1935 they had established an architectural practice in Wilmington. Enthusiastic proponents of the International Style, the couple found Victorine's ancestral state tradition-bound. They accommodated, working within the traditional vernacular, and by 1939 had achieved enough success to purchase 17 acres outside Wilmington, where they built their house, undiluted by the family passion for historicism.

An architectural integration of family and business, their single-story frame house, one of the first modernist houses in the neighborhood, wrapped around an informal courtyard entrance. On one side was the service wing (powder room, kitchen with pantry, walk-in cold storage, porch, maid's room, bathroom, storage, and garage), with the central, flexible-plan living room-dining room in the middle. The bedroom wing was on the other side (master, guest, two children's rooms, three bathrooms, and a playroom). Extending from the master bedroom was an architectural studio, one of the largest rooms

TULIP HOLLOW

Dining room. The painting of Coleman du Pont Homsey is by Henriette Wyeth Hurd, ca. 1940.

in the house. Its north wall had a large glass window that provided consistent natural light throughout the day. Located off their bedroom, the studio allowed the Homseys to work long into the night without disturbing their children. The double fireplace adjoining the bedroom wall and studio wall reflected the balance of the couple's relationship.

Victorine belonged to the Garden Club of Wilmington and was a passionate horticulturist whose expertise was landscape design. The Homseys designed planting pockets for the south-facing courtyard windows. Their two sons, Coleman (born in 1934) and Eldon (born in 1936), are the subjects of portraits by Henriette Wyeth Hurd, sister of Andrew Wyeth. The paintings formed the primary decoration in the dining room and living room, which could be made into one large space by opening three sliding panels. According to the September 1940 issue of *Architectural Forum,* in which the house was featured, the interior walls were painted dusty pink and gray-white, a color scheme based on Hurd's painting of young Coleman.

A tenant house on their property was inhabited by Lucius Baylor, the chauffeur/gardener, his wife, and two sons. The house, although considerably smaller, was similar in design to the main residence, with open porches on both sides of the single-story frame house. Baylor's house appeared in the June 1944 issue of *Architectural Forum,* which presented it as a model of budget building ("Total cost including adjacent garage-shed was $3,450").

The Homseys sold Tulip Hollow to family members in 1962.

Planting pocket, ca. 1940

Master bedroom terrace, with studio window on the right, ca. 1940

TULIP HOLLOW

Studio, ca. 1940

Tenant house, ca. 1940

TULIP HOLLOW

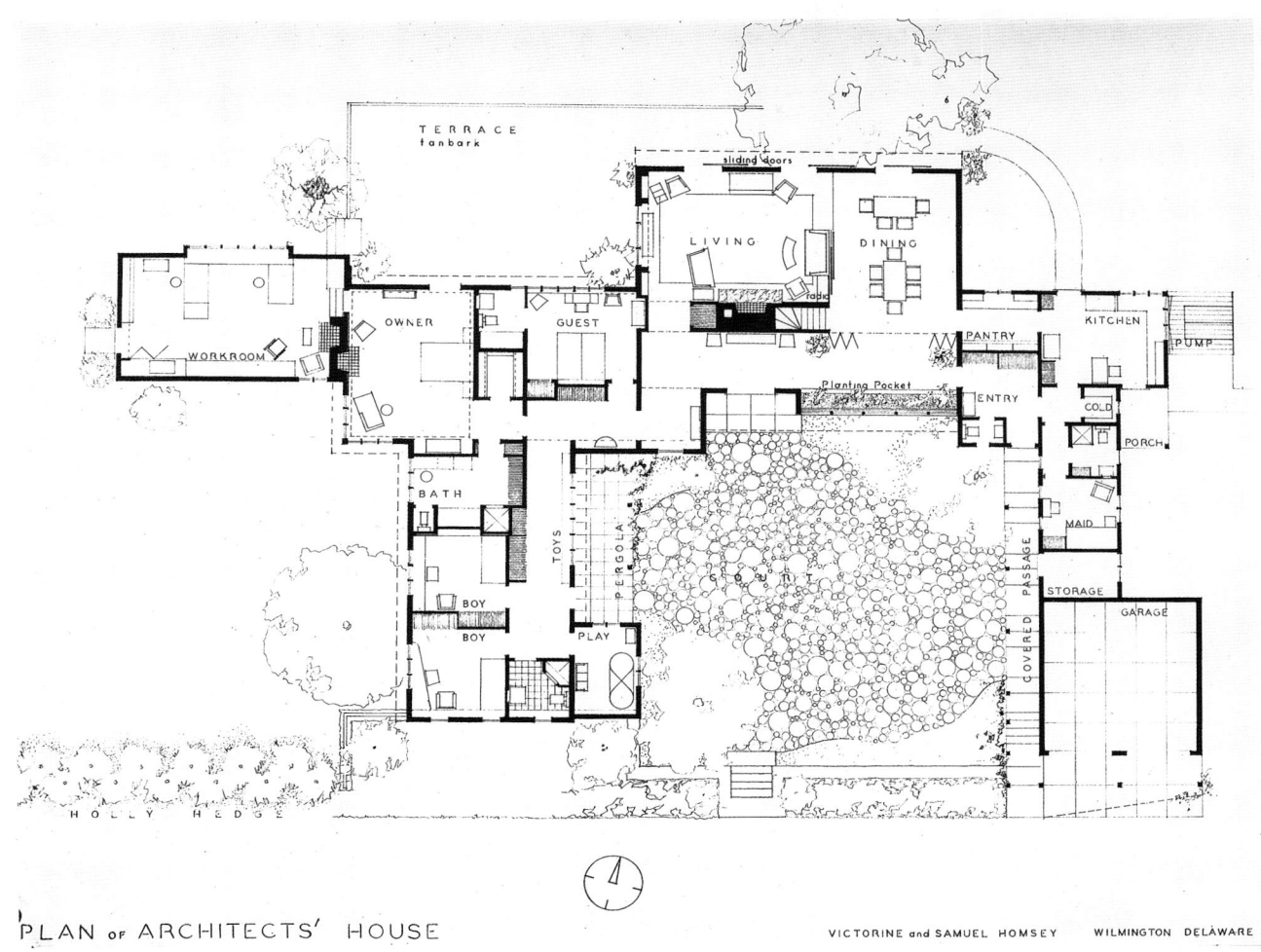

Floor plan, ca. 1939

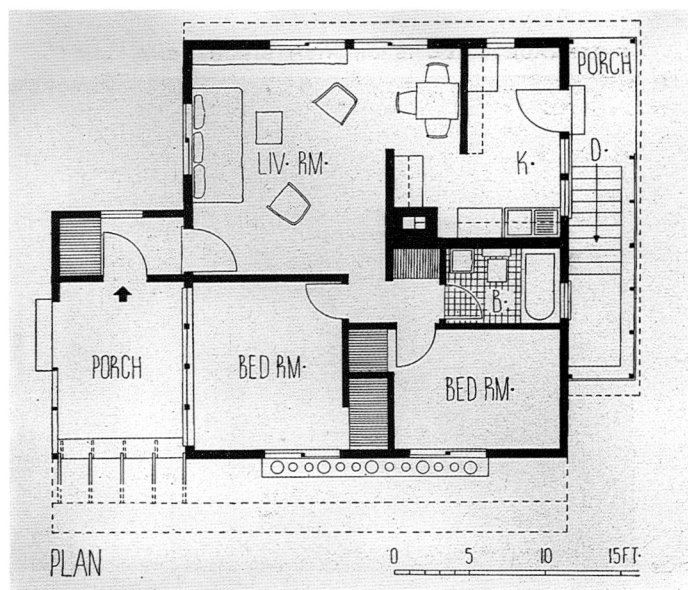

Tenant house floor plan, 1940

THE COTTAGE AT WINTERTHUR
1950–51

Residence of Henry Francis du Pont

The Cottage, ca. 1979

THE COTTAGE AT WINTERTHUR

The Cottage, ca. 1955

IN 1950 HENRY FRANCIS "HARRY" DU PONT wrote to his friend Eugene Grace, chairman of the board of Bethlehem Steel Corporation: "We are leaving our house here in January as it is to be made into a museum and I have been building a small house at the foot of the lawn . . . I ordered steel long before Korea . . . I am really getting quite desperate." Grace solved the problem but asked: "I like your emphasis on 'small house.' Are you black marketing this steel?" Du Pont replied: "In order that you may not have any doubts (about my activities) perhaps I should say that my house is a big small house."

H. F. du Pont's "big small" house was constructed on the site of the original estate Cottage, which had been built in 1838 for Evelina du Pont and her husband, Antoine Bidermann. Evelina and Antoine occupied the Cottage between 1839 and 1841 while their residence at Winterthur—the estate they named after the Swiss ancestral home of the Bidermann family—was under construction. After they moved into their new home, the Cottage housed estate workers until 1902, when Henry Algernon du Pont and his family lived there for two years while they expanded the main residence built by the Bidermanns. Between 1928 and 1931 Harry du Pont, his wife, Ruth, and their two children, the third generation at Winterthur, also took up residence in the Cottage when the main house was enlarged yet again.

Front door to the Cottage, ca. 1955

Entrance hall, ca. 1965

By the start of World War II, the du Pont home at Winterthur was nine stories high and contained more than 140 rooms. It was furnished with a collection of American decorative arts that surpassed those in the American Wing at the Metropolitan Museum of Art. Harry had long planned for his showplace to become a museum after his death, but the war changed everything. By the late 1940s most rooms were closed up, and the building was impossible to heat or staff. Harry, therefore, revamped his plans. He accelerated the schedule for opening his museum by hiring a professional curator and photographer to document his collection. And because tax concerns dictated that he move out of his home before the museum opened, he and Ruth took refuge in the Cottage.

At first Harry wanted simply to modify the old Cottage, but he quickly realized that the 1838 structure had extensive water damage. He wrote to a friend, "Much to my joy . . . the whole house was practically falling apart, so we tore it down." He and architect Thomas Waterman, who had installed historic architecture in the main Winterthur house, decided to build something new. It was the first time they had worked together without the constraints of historical precedents. What they created was a clean-line, English Regency–style villa.

Harry, then 68 years old, had already built three houses. He knew exactly what he needed in his new home, but in the late 1940s building materials were in short supply, of inferior quality, and terribly expensive. "Everything costs so much that it is almost driving me crazy," he wrote. Du Pont pressed his former prep school classmate Grace for steel and resorted to recycling for much of the rest. As bathrooms,

Living room, ca. 1965

cupboards, and closets were removed from the main Winterthur residence in the course of converting the spaces to period rooms, the fixtures, lights, and extraneous doors were installed in the Cottage. Mantels, fanlights, and other architectural elements that had been in storage were pulled out and reused.

The Cottage area in which the du Ponts lived was compact: a conservatory, living room, sitting room, and dining room occupied the first floor; their bedrooms were on the second. There were six guest rooms and two large rooms in the basement for entertaining the grandchildren. A front elevator served the family; the staff used a back elevator in addition to

H. F. du Pont's office, ca. 1965

a dumbwaiter. The rest of the house—more than half the square footage—was devoted to service and storage space.

The architectural mélange created in the Cottage by the use of recycled materials was most obvious in the du Ponts' bedroom suites, which were identical to those in the museum, though on a smaller scale. Harry had a bedroom, office, bath, and dressing room; Ruth's suite contained a bedroom, bath, and dressing room. The hall between their suites was ornamented with recycled antique hardware, wallpaper, and fanlights. A fireplace surround and shell cabinet deemed unsuitable for the museum because they were English found a new home in Harry's office. The dining room was created around a set of

H. F. du Pont's office, ca. 1965

Aubusson tapestries that had once hung in the New York apartment that the du Ponts sold in 1942.[1] Most of the furniture in the Cottage was from the apartment. Since the majority of pieces were French, Italian, and English, it enabled Harry and Ruth to live with familiar things and continue to buy items for the Cottage without competing in the marketplace for objects for their newly founded museum of American decorative arts.

The Cottage at Winterthur was Thomas Waterman's final creation. A pioneer in historic preservation, he is best known as an author and for his restoration work for the National Park Service and at Williamsburg. However, he also designed new buildings, and his client list included Robert Woods and Mildred Bliss, founders of Dumbarton Oaks Research Center; collectors Colonel Edgar and Bernice Chrysler Garbisch; and

THE COTTAGE AT WINTERTHUR

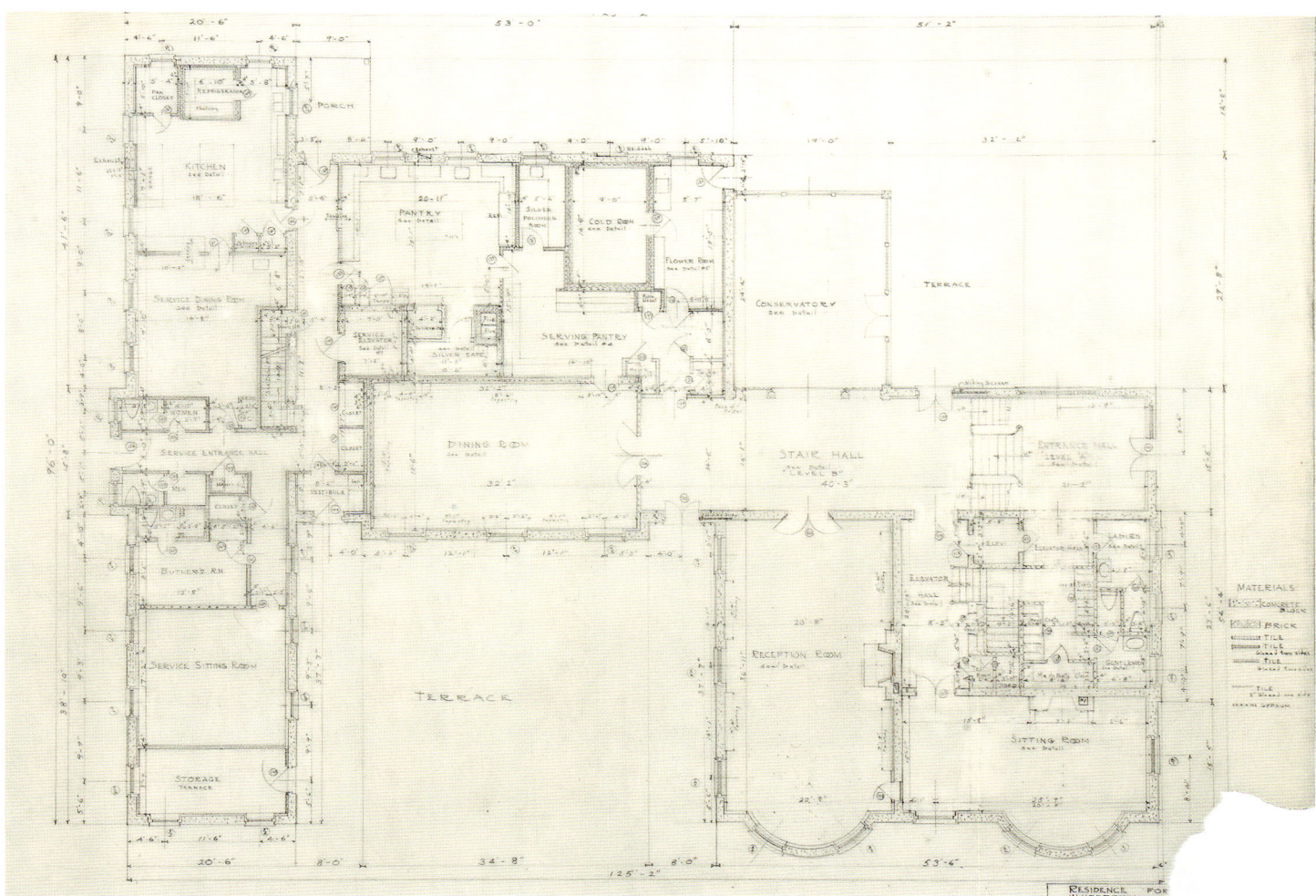

First floor plan, ca. 1980

Mrs. Warren Delano Robbins, who decorated U.S. embassies around the world in the 1930s and 1940s. Ten of his 12 new buildings were masonry, with such formal features as parquet floors, cove moldings, and double doors. His houses tend to be well-integrated into the surrounding landscape, characteristics exemplified in the Cottage at Winterthur.

The simple garden around the Cottage was designed by Marian Coffin. By planting a witch hazel bush on the terrace and putting in a single set of steps for potted plants, Coffin re-created, in miniature, some of Harry's favorite garden elements, just as Waterman re-created favorite features of the main house (a conservatory, walk-through dressing room, and double flower rooms).

Since the time of Ruth du Pont's death in 1967 and Harry's in 1969, the Cottage has housed staff offices as well as the Winterthur Museum Store.

PORTFOLIO OF HOUSES

Upper Louviers

UPPER LOUVIERS, 1700s, 1802, New Castle County, Delaware
OWNERS: DuPont Company; Alfred I. du Pont; the Nemours Foundation
ARCHITECT: Alfred Victor du Pont (additions and renovation, 1833, 1837); Francis McIntire (1936)
BUILDER: James Smyth (1901)
Demolished 1978

E. I. du Pont bought this four-room stone farmhouse in 1802 and enlarged it before 1833. In 1837 his daughter Sophie Madeline and her husband and first cousin, Admiral Samuel Francis DuPont, made it their home. Sophie's brother Alfred Victor renovated the house for them, turning it into a Greek Revival residence with a columned front porch and spiral interior staircase. Mary Alicia Bradford, a great-granddaughter of E. I. du Pont, moved into the house with her first husband, George Amory Maddox, in 1901. They made changes, mostly in the service areas and plumbing arrangements. The Maddoxes divorced in 1908, and Alicia married Alfred I. du Pont. In 1918 Alicia encouraged her first cousin Francis I. du Pont to move into the house. Francis I and his family lived there until 1972 although it was owned by Alfred, who inherited the property after Alicia's 1920 death. According to Francis's daughter Elise du Pont Elrick, who wrote an architectural history of the house in 1970, her father added an octagonal room in 1936. He also built a miniature railroad track in the yard for a four-foot high electric train. There were two aquariums, one outside and one inside, both stocked with fish. The house was razed in 1978, and the land is now part of the DuPont Country Club.

Hagley House

HAGLEY HOUSE, 1814, New Castle County, Delaware
OWNERS: DuPont Company; Henry Belin du Pont
ARCHITECT: Eleuthère Irénée du Pont
Demolished 1952

This house bore the name of the surrounding area, Hagley. One of two frame DuPont houses, it was built by E. I. du Pont for his brother-in-law Charles Dalmas and was home to E. I.'s daughter Evelina and her husband, Antoine, and later to E. I.'s youngest son, Alexis I. du Pont, who died there after an 1857 explosion. Mrs. Lammot du Pont and her children lived at Hagley House the summer of 1885 after her husband died in an explosion. Considerably damaged in the 1890 blast, the house was reconstructed, but a 1915 powder accident made it completely uninhabitable. Henry Belin du Pont bought it from the DuPont Company in 1922. In the 1920s and 1930s, Mary du Pont Laird and her son, William Winder "Chick" Laird Jr., took up some of the floorboards to reuse at Lower Louviers. In 1974 the property was deeded to the Hagley Foundation.

Hagley (Jacob Broom) House

HAGLEY (JACOB BROOM) HOUSE, ca. 1794, 1823, New Castle County, Delaware
OWNERS: Jacob Broom; John Hirons; DuPont Company; Irene S. du Pont; Mariana du Pont and her husband, Henry Harper Silliman
ARCHITECT: Robeson Lea Perot (renovations, 1896); Victorine and Samuel Homsey (renovations, 1937–38); Albert Kruse (renovations, 1952–53). Builder: James Smyth (ca. 1900)
Private residence

This house was built for Jacob Broom, a signer of the U.S. Constitution. In 1823 E. I. du Pont bought the house and rented it to family members. His daughter Eleuthera and her husband, Thomas Mackie Smith, occupied the house from 1839 to 1873, and Francis G. du Pont and his wife, Elise Wigfall Simons, lived there from 1874 to 1919. They made considerable changes between 1879 and 1893, including the addition of a conservatory with balconies and the transformation of the grapery into a billiard room and the grain-storage builing into a chemical laboratory with an astronomical observatory. In 1887 the house became one of the first to be electrified in Delaware. After Elise's death in 1919, the DuPont Company took over the property. In 1933 Irene S. du Pont, one of Francis G.'s children, bought it for her daughter Mariana, who stripped off most of the late 19th-century additions. The Homseys built a caretaker's cottage in 1937–38. Hagley is still family owned.

Rokeby

ROKEBY, 1836, New Castle County, Delaware
OWNERS: DuPont Company; T. Coleman du Pont; Alice du Pont Wilson Buck; Dorcas Van Dyke Farquhar
ARCHITECT: Unknown
Private residence

Rokeby, named after an 1812 Sir Walter Scott poem, was built for Gabrielle Josephine du Pont at the time of her marriage to William Breck. The floor plan was based on Upper Louviers, where Gabrielle had been living at the time of her marriage. A mistake in measurement made the house smaller than intended. The Brecks lived at Rokeby until they moved to Scranton, Pennsylvania, in 1859. Gabrielle's first cousin Charles I. du Pont Jr. took on the house about the time of his marriage to his second cousin Mary Sophie du Pont in 1862. A succession of his relations lived there in the 19th century, including his sister Mary Van Dyke du Pont, who died there in 1909. T. Coleman du Pont then bought Rokeby. E. Paul du Pont and his wife, Jean Kane Foulke, lived in the house while their home, the Second Office, was being readied. Rokeby was given to T. Coleman's daughter Alice on her marriage to Paul E. Wilson in 1912. Wilson died in World War I, and Alice lived at Rokeby after her marriage to C. Douglass Buck in 1921, until they moved to Buena Vista in 1930. In the early 1930s, Henry Belin du Pont and his wife rented Rokeby while their Okie-designed house was being built on the Red Clay Creek. Dorcas Van Dyke Buck, Alice and C. Douglass Buck's daughter, was given the house in 1943. She enlarged it and lived there with her husband Donald Farquhar until 1978. It is still in the family.

SWAMP HALL, ca. 1800?, 1864, New Castle County, Delaware
OWNERS: DuPont Company; Alfred I. du Pont
ARCHITECT: Unknown
Demolished 1910

Swamp Hall

According to P. S. du Pont's memoirs, Swamp Hall was "an old house" where Dr. John P. Wales lived until his wife Louisa Belin died in childbirth in April 1858. E. I. du Pont II, his wife, Charlotte, and their two (soon to be five) children moved to Swamp Hall in 1864. A large addition increased the size of the house to 13 rooms by the 1870s. The children continued to live there after being orphaned in 1877. The oldest son, Alfred I., resided in the house with his wife, Bessie, until their 1907 divorce. In 1910, he evicted Bessie and demolished the residence.

Goodstay

GOODSTAY, ca. 1740, 1868, Wilmington, Delaware
OWNERS: Multiple owners until Margaretta du Pont in 1868; Emma Pauline du Pont; T. Coleman du Pont; Ellen du Pont and her first husband, Hollyday S. Meeds Jr., and second husband, Robert Wheelwright
ARCHITECT: Edmond Gilchrist (alterations, 1924–37). Builder: J. S. Cornell & Son Inc. Landscape architect: Wheelwright & Stevenson
Currently part of the University of Delaware, Wilmington campus

Originally known as Green Hill, this was the childhood home of artist Howard Pyle. In 1868 Margaretta du Pont, widow of Alfred V. and family matriarch, moved into the house and changed the name to Goodstay, an anglicized version of the du Pont family's first American residence, Bon Sejours. Ellen du Pont Meeds Wheelwright greatly enlarged the house and developed the grounds into fulsome Colonial Revival gardens. *The Architectural Record* (January 1929) featured Goodstay as "a remodeled and enlarged farmhouse," and *Landscape Architecture* (October 1929) presented "the Garden at Goodstay."

Vireaux

VIREAUX, 1877, New Castle County, Delaware
OWNERS: Victorine du Pont and her husband, A. Lentilhon Foster; Evelyn Irving
ARCHITECT: Theophilus Parsons Chandler (1876); Bissell & Perot (alterations, 1902) Builder: Elmer Humphries (1935)
Demolished

The nine-acre Vireaux property, originally part of the Winterthur estate, was given to Victorine du Pont on her marriage to A. Lentilhon Foster. The name Vireaux derives from the Lentilhon ancestral town in France. The stable and gate lodge, designed by Chandler, were of dark gray Brandywine granite. The tall, 18-room frame residence included a conservatory, library, and spacious front hall decorated with mounted trophy heads and taxidermy bird specimens in a glass case. The conservatory was supported by two greenhouses located south of the house. The garden was naturalistic; native trees and wild flowers, especially trilliums, were encouraged. Victorine left Vireaux to her nephew Evelyn Irving, who demolished the house . The farmland was later developed into residential housing. The original Chandler-designed stable, gatehouse, and water tower survive.

Crooked Billet

CROOKED BILLET, 1682 foundation and hearth, 18th-century inn, 1878, Wilmington, Delaware
OWNERS: Multiple owners; William du Pont; William du Pont Jr.; Jean Ellen du Pont and second husband, James Hoge Tyler McConnell
ARCHITECT: Unknown (alterations, 1938)
Private residence

In 1878 this 30-acre property, called the Brindley Farm, was part of William du Pont's Pelleport. Twentieth-century additions flank the original portion of the house, which was once an inn known as the Crooked Billet. William du Pont Jr. renovated the house in 1938 and gave it to his daughter Jean Ellen when she was widowed in 1943. On the National Register of Historic Places, it is still owned by family members.

Rencourt

RENCOURT, 1890, New Castle County, Delaware
OWNERS: Alexis Irénée du Pont and his second wife, Elizabeth Canby Bradford
ARCHITECT: Theophilus Parsons Chandler (1890); Robeson Lea Perot (alterations, 1899)
Demolished 1950s

The heavy-looking stone house, built of Brandywine granite, was named for the first wife of P. S. du Pont de Nemours—Nicole Charlotte Marie Louise Le Dée de Rencourt. The residence had deep porches, a mansard roof, and an oval-shaped conservatory off the library. Four family houses were built nearby: Valmy, the Porter Schutt house, Dogwood, and Doggone.

LYNDHAM, 1901, New Castle County, Delaware
OWNER: Evelina du Pont
ARCHITECT: Bissell & Perot
Private residence

Lyndham was one of the first true Colonial Revival houses in Wilmington. The building details are a combination of poured concrete and terra-cotta rather than limestone. Evelina du Pont was the favorite maiden aunt to dozens of nieces and nephews. Her generosity and good humor made Lyndham a favorite gathering spot for the family. The house is no longer owned by the family.

Lyndham

POINT LOOKOUT, ca. 1902, New Castle County, Delaware
OWNERS: DuPont Company; Francis G. du Pont; A. Felix du Pont; Lydia du Pont
ARCHITECT: Unknown
Private residence

Point Lookout

In 1902 Francis G. du Pont bought this farm on the Brandywine River after he retired from the DuPont Company. Prior to World War I, his sons formed the Ball Grain Explosives Company and conducted experiments at Point Lookout Farm. His granddaughter Lydia improved the house, providing electricity, plumbing, a new addition, and a swimming pool. The farm is still family owned.

VALMY, ca. 1906, New Castle County, Delaware
OWNERS: Alice Eugenie du Pont and her husband, Julien de Villiers Ortiz; Marie Alexia du Pont Ortiz de Bie
ARCHITECT: Unknown
Demolished

This exotic-looking, 30-room house was a wedding present to poet Alice Eugenie du Pont (*The Witch of Endor*, 1937; *The Scene Shifter*, 1939) on her marriage to Julien de Villiers Ortiz. It was named after the 1792 Battle of Valmy. In 1959 daughter Marie Alexia du Pont Ortiz de Bie gave Valmy to the Psychosynthesis Research Foundation, a nonprofit organization of which she was president. The foundation sold Valmy a year after de Bie's death in 1963, and the house was razed.

Valmy

THOMAS FRANCIS BAYARD HOUSE, 1908, Wilmington, Delaware
OWNERS: Senator Thomas Francis Bayard and his wife, Elizabeth Bradford du Pont
ARCHITECT: Charles Barton Keen
Private residence

This city house, still owned by the family, overlooks Rockford Park. Bayard was the fourth generation in his family to be U.S. Senator from Delaware, serving from November 1921 to March 1929. The house was featured in the February 1908 issue of *Brickbuilder*. The facade is based on Mount Clare (1760), the Baltimore, Maryland, home of Charles Carroll.

Thomas Francis Bayard House

BROOKDALE FARM, ca. 1800, ca. 1910, New Castle County, Delaware
OWNERS: T. Coleman du Pont; Walter S. Carpenter Jr.; Walter S. Carpenter III and his wife, Murton du Pont
ARCHITECT: Clarence R. Hope (alterations, 1930); Victorine and Samuel Homsey (alterations and addition, 1941)
Private residence

This land was part of T. Coleman du Pont's Old Mill property. Holstein cows were bred at Brookdale in the 1910s under the direction of A. Bidermann du Pont. Walter S. Carpenter Jr., later a president of the DuPont Company, purchased the 171-acre Brookdale Farm in 1927. The property was divided, and Carpenter's son, Walter Samuel Carpenter III, made Brookdale Farm his home when he married Elizabeth Murton du Pont in 1938. The house and property are still in the family.

Mrs. Victor du Pont House

MRS. VICTOR DU PONT HOUSE, ca. 1911, New Castle County, Delaware
OWNERS: Victor du Pont Jr. and his wife, Josephine Anderson
ARCHITECT: Unknown. Landscape architects: Lewis & Valentine (ca. 1911)
Private residence

In 1908 Victor du Pont Jr. purchased 98.5 acres outside Wilmington. He died in 1911, leaving the property to his wife, who created a large garden around the house. The house has been sold outside the family, and most of the land is now part of the Bidermann Country Club, owned by Winterthur Corporation.

Hotel Du Pont

HOTEL DU PONT, 1911–12, Wilmington, Delaware
OWNER: DuPont Company
ARCHITECT: Frederick Godley and J. Andre Fouilhoux.
INTERIOR DESIGN: Joel Barber and Raymond Hood

This extant luxury hotel, part of the new vision of the DuPont Company, is attached to the corporate office building in downtown Wilmington. P. S. du Pont maintained an apartment in the hotel his entire life. At the time it opened in January 1913, it was said to have cost more per room than any other hotel in the world. The building was doubled in size in 1917. Nylon was invented at the DuPont Company in 1937, and by 1948 the Nylon Suite at the hotel, decorated by Joanne Seybold, had upholstery, carpeting, lampshades, and towels all made of the material.

Archibald M. L. du Pont House

ARCHIBALD M. L. DU PONT HOUSE, 1913, New Castle County, Delaware
OWNERS: Archibald M. L. du Pont and his wife, Elizabeth Hayward
ARCHITECT: Robeson Lea Perot
Private residence

This house on the outskirts of Wilmington originally sat on 56 acres. It is one of four, possibly five, houses that Perot built for Elizabeth du Pont's siblings. The house was sold after Elizabeth's death in 1973, and the land was developed.

BUENA VISTA, 1847, 1914, New Castle County, Delaware
OWNERS: John Clayton; Douglass family; T. Coleman du Pont; Alice du Pont and her husband, C. Douglass Buck
ARCHITECT: R. Brognard Okie (library wing with master bedroom, 1930–32); Victorine and Samuel Homsey (pool and pool house, 1937)

In 1914 T. Coleman du Pont purchased Buena Vista. His daughter Alice married C. Douglass Buck, a descendent of the original builders of the house, and they lived there after Buck became governor of Delaware in 1929. The Bucks sold Buena Vista to the state in 1965 for one dollar. The house, now on the Register of Historic Houses, currently serves as a state conference center.

Buena Vista

DOGWOOD, 1917–18, New Castle County, Delaware
OWNERS: Eugene E. du Pont and his wife, Catherine Dulcinea Moxham
ARCHITECT: Unknown, possibly the owners
Demolished 1966

Dogwood

The style of this house was unusual, a variant of an octagonal Federal shape with cast concrete exterior walls and a flat red roof that was used as a skating rink. Inside and out, the house mixed Federal Revival details with heavy rustic stonework. The property had a working farm with crops, horses, kennels, a fully stocked dovecote, and the houses of two du Pont daughters: Dulcinea Ophelia Payne du Pont and her husband, George Tyler Weymouth, owned Doggone, ca. 1930; and Phyllis Moxham du Pont and her husband, Charles Porter Schutt, resided in a ca. 1935 residence designed by Jim Thompson. These houses survive and are owned by family members.

DILWYNE FARMS, 1922–25, New Castle County, Delaware
OWNERS: Margaretta Lammot du Pont and her husband, Robert Ruliph Morgan Carpenter
ARCHITECT: Brown & Whiteside (1922); Albert Spahr (alterations, 1925). Metalwork: Samuel Yellin (1922, 1925)
Demolished

The residence at Dilwyne Farms was a modified modern French style with a red tile deck atop hip roof, stuccoed walls, and glass casement doors leading out to the formal garden terrace. The property had a dairy, a steer farm, stables, kennels for breeding Chesapeake Bay retrievers, a private movie theatre, ice skating rink, tennis court, greenhouse range, eight tenant houses, and a fire engine in the garage in case of emergency. In her 1932 *Gardens in America*, Marion Cran wrote, "Mrs. R. R. M. Carpenter has one of the nicest swimming pools I saw in America, beautifully placed among green lawns and trees; the whole garden is of good taste, planned with a large gesture, free and simple." The family has built a new house on the land.

Dilwyne Farms

STRAND MILLAS, 1701, 1923, ca. 1930, New Castle County, Delaware
OWNERS: Gregg family; DuPont Company; Henry Algernon du Pont; Henry Francis du Pont; Louisa d'Andelot Carpenter
ARCHITECT: Unknown
Private residence

The oldest house west of the Brandywine, this 1701 structure, which is on the National Register of Historic Places, was named by the Gregg family. In 1923 Henry Algernon du Pont folded the main house, a later 19th-century tenant house, stable, and stone barn into his Winterthur estate. Strand Millas was purchased from H. F. du Pont for Louisa d'Andelot Carpenter at the time of her short-lived marriage to John King Jenney (1929–31). A charismatic woman, Louisa was an accomplished equestrienne, the first woman master of the hounds in the United States, and a Broadway producer. She renovated the house and barn and entertained her friends, including Tallulah Bankhead, Clifton Webb, and Libby Holman. The photo shows a contemporary view as restored by the current owners, Dr. and Mrs. Ronald Finch.

Strand Millas

SQUIRREL RUN, 1926, New Castle County, Delaware
OWNERS: S. Hallock du Pont and first wife, Elizabeth Wrenn, and second wife, Virginia Simmons
ARCHITECT: R. Brognard Okie. Metalwork: Samuel Yellin.
Private residence

Squirrel Run

This house, on former DuPont Company land, is among the largest of the Okie-designed houses in Wilmington. The 80-acre property included a gate house, several tenant houses, tennis court, swimming pool, and remnants of old mill buildings, including a blacksmith and machine shop. The mill buildings are now owned by Hagley Museum. The remainder of the property has been sold out of the family.

CRAWFORD GREENEWALT HOUSE, ca. 1929, Wilmington, Delaware
OWNERS: Margaretta du Pont and her husband, Crawford Greenewalt
ARCHITECT: Albert Ely Ives. Builder: A. L. Lauritsen
Private residence

The 1930s French-style house was of stucco and limestone with exaggerated quoins, a green slate roof, and an arched entrance door. There was a greenhouse in the garden for orchids. The house was sold out of the family by 1940.

Crawford Greenewalt House

CALMAR, ca. 1930, New Castle County, Delaware
OWNERS: Albert Ely Ives; Alfred Victor du Pont
ARCHITECT: Albert Ely Ives (ca. 1930); Alfred Victor du Pont (1939); Victorine and Samuel Homsey (renovations, 1980s). Builder: A. L. Lauritsen (1930)
Private residence

The house was the residence of architect Albert Ely Ives until he moved to Hawaii in 1935. It was subsequently purchased by Alfred Victor du Pont and is still owned by the family.

Calmar

PORTFOLIO OF HOUSES

Doggone

DOGGONE, ca. 1930, New Castle County, Delaware
OWNERS: Dulcinea Ophelia Payne du Pont and her husband, George Tyler Weymouth
ARCHITECT: Unknown. Builder: A. L. Lauritsen
Private residence

Doggone was built on Alexis I. du Pont's Rencourt property, not far from Dulcinea's (known as Deo) parent's house, Dogwood. The house is still owned by the family.

Dauneport

DAUNEPORT, 1933, New Castle County, Delaware
OWNERS: Amy E. du Pont; Eugene du Pont III
ARCHITECT: Mary Craig, Santa Barbara, California. Builder: G. W. McCauley & Son
Private residence

Dauneport was modeled on Mount Vernon. Amy du Pont also had a house in Santa Barbara called Casa del Sueno, which had cactus-inspired interiors by the Herter Brothers. By 1949 she had given Dauneport to her nephew Eugene du Pont III, but it is no longer owned by family members. Plans and drawings for the house are in the Mary Craig Collection at the Library of Congress.

H. B. DU PONT HOUSE, 1934, New Castle County, Delaware
OWNER: Henry Belin du Pont and first wife, Margaret Wilson Lewis, and second wife, Emily Tybout du Pont
ARCHITECT: R. Brognard Okie
Private residence

Situated high on a hill overlooking the Red Clay Creek, the house is still owned by the family.

H. B. du Pont House

LIMERICK, 1815, 1934, New Castle County, Delaware
OWNER: Mary Belin Laird and her husband, Ellason Downs
ARCHITECT: Victorine and Samuel Homsey (addition, 1936)
Private residence

Originally just four rooms, the house was given by Mary Alletta Belin du Pont Laird to her daughter Mary (known as Molly) shortly after her 1934 marriage to Ellason Downs. In 1936 Mrs. Laird hired the Homseys to design a large stucco addition to the original stone farmhouse. The name derives from the county in Ireland where the Downs family originated. Limerick, now called Foxspring, is still owned by the family.

Limerick

Letdown

LETDOWN, 1935, New Castle County, Delaware
Owner: Alletta d'Andelot Laird and her husband, Robert Norton Downs III
Architect: Victorine and Samuel Homsey
Private residence

Mary Alletta Belin du Pont Laird gave this four-bedroom, three-bath stone house to her daughter Alletta on her marriage. The 1935 date stone on the whitewashed house is prominently encircled with red brick. The service wing to the right of the front door was well organized, complete with a staff dining room. The land, owned by the family and originally part of an apple orchard, is now in conservation trust.

Bois-des-Fossés

BOIS-DES-FOSSÉS, 1936–40, Wilmington, Delaware
Owners: Pierre S. du Pont III and his wife, Jane Holcomb
Architect: Massena & du Pont. Landscape architect: Frederick Holcomb (1939) Plantsmen: Lewis & Valentine, under the supervision of Ferrucio Vitale (1939)
Currently known as Brantwyn, owned by the DuPont Country Club

The slate-roof, Georgian-style house is one of the few brick houses built by a du Pont. Brantwyn serves as a wedding facility and conference center.

WAGONER'S ROW, 1938, New Castle County, Delaware
Owners: DuPont Company; R. R. M. Carpenter Jr. and his wife, Mary Kaye Phelps
Architect: John Mullins. Builder: Di Sabatino.
Landscape Architect: Noel Chamberlin
Private residence

In the 19th century, row houses were constructed here for DuPont Company wagon drivers. The Carpenters lived in one of the houses while their new home was being built. Two of the original houses survive; one is a tenant house and the other is a garage.

Wagoner's Row

RIDGELY, 1940, New Castle County, Delaware
Owners: Nicholas du Pont and his wife, Genevieve "Bunny" Estes
Architect: R. Brognard Okie
Private residence

Bunny du Pont, president of the Garden Club of America from 1973 to 1975, created spectacular gardens at Ridgely. She also maintained a greenhouse of rare plants, including the blue Himalayan poppy and night-blooming cereus. The pool house, an integral part of the garden, was decorated with Pennsylvania German chalkware. The property is still family owned.

NOTES

INTRODUCTION

1. In the early days, the Brandywine River was more often referred to as a creek. Both terms appear throughout this publication.

2. Antoine Bidermann, December 8, 1864, commented on Brandywine French, see Longwood Mss, Group 4, Box 2, Hagley Museum & Library. None of Henry's children held title to the houses in which they lived (with the exception of Ellen du Pont Irving at Sunnyside) until after his death in 1889, at which time they inherited under the terms of his will. Pierre Samuel du Pont, *Life in My Father's House*, ed. H. Rodney Sharp Jr. (Wilmington, DE: H. Rodney Sharp Jr., 1987).

3. Joseph Frazier Wall, *Alfred I. du Pont: The Man and His Family* (New York: Oxford University Press, 1990), p. 127. Cleveland Moffat, "Life and Work in the Powder Mills," *McClure's Magazine* 5, no. 1 (June 1895); APS Online, 2–17, p. 2.

4. The translation of the name is Wood of the Trenches, a reference to nearby Roman ruins. Although P. S. du Pont II was interested in Bois-des-Fossés when the house came up for sale in 1929, he didn't buy it. He wrote to his brother-in-law Lammot Belin, "It is possible it may fall into my hands but… it is just an ordinary little house in the country with very little attraction" (P. S. du Pont Papers, 1929, Chateau D'Andelot files, Hagley Museum & Library). A wealth of material on Bois-des-Fossés is housed at Hagley. Winterthur also has archival material, mostly descriptions of visits (Henry Algernon in 1875; Henry Francis in 1906) and the 1846 watercolor Smith's husband made during their visit (acc. 1970.1354).

5. Eleutherian Mills was named after Eleuthère Irénée du Pont, whose first name was derived from the Greek *Eleutheros* "liberty" and *Eirene* "peace." The 1868 obituary for Louise G. du Pont, a daughter of Boss Henry, states she died at Nemours; P. S. du Pont Papers, Box 253, File 369, Hagley Museum & Library. In the 1860s Henry du Pont wrote to his son Henry Algernon from Nemours, see letter dated April 7, 1867, Group 7, Box 5, Series B, Hagley Museum & Library. Henry du Pont's obituary simply states he died at his unnamed country residence; see Acc. 471, C, 47, Hagley Museum & Library. A September 23, 1907, letter from T. Coleman du Pont to J. P. Laffey announced how houses should be designated and includes Nemours and Eleutherian Mills. Possibly this is when the name was adopted for Nemours and also Eleutherian Mills reverted to its name; Elsie's letter is in T. Coleman du Pont Papers, Acc. 1075, File 24, Hagley Museum & Library. To confuse matters more, A. I. du Pont decided that his 1909 mansion should be called Nemours. W8-40073, Hagley Museum & Library.

6. Swamp Hall shows up in the 1816 survey of company houses; Allan J. Henry, *The Life of Alexis I. du Pont*, vol. 2 (Philadelphia: William F. Fell Co., 1945), p. 33. My thanks to Marjorie McNinch. See also Du Pont, *Life in My Father's House*, p. 33, and Wall, *Alfred I. du Pont*, pp. 107, 114. Other amusing du Pont family house names include Dripping Spigots, Letdown, and Belly Acres.

7. The partnership houses were Eleutherian Mills, Upper and Lower Louviers, Nemours, Hagley, Hagley House, Rokeby, and Swamp Hall. By 1900 Eleutherian Mills was a clubhouse and Upper and Lower Louviers were boarded up. See the letter from Lammot du Pont to George Patton, February 23, 1907, in which he describes them all as "in poor shape" (T. Coleman du Pont Papers, Acc. 1075, File 24, Hagley Museum & Library); see also Thomas Coleman du Pont's open letter to the family, April 8, 1914, quoted in the chapter on Old Nemours, Acc. 1503, Box 11, Hagley Museum & Library. "Plan for Taking Care of Brandywine Real Estate and Tenement and Farm Houses, Effective January 1, 1906" (T. Coleman du Pont Papers, Acc.

1075, File 24, Hagley Museum & Library). An independent surveyor assigned values to the properties. Coleman had large landholdings around Wilmington not including the farm or his town house. He owned Goodstay, Buena Vista, and Rokeby, all of which he bequeathed to his daughters. Part of Coleman's land may have been bought from the company. Pierre's Longwood real estate had a separate history although company records indicate he purchased company land in Wilmington as well; T. Coleman du Pont Papers, Acc. 1075, File 24, Hagley Museum & Library. Frances Gurney du Pont purchased Point Lookout in 1902, but the lack of pretension and plumbing suggest a simple working farm rather than an estate.

8. Alfred D. Chandler Jr. and Stephen Salsbury, *Pierre S. du Pont and the Making of the Modern Corporation* (New York: Harper & Row, 1971), pp. 359–60. John Mosher, "Will They Be the Richest Family in the World?" *Every Week* (August 14, 1916). Victorine du Pont Foster Scrapbook, Acc. 471, Series C, Box 43, Hagley Museum & Library.

9. Almost every nonprofit organization in Delaware has taken advantage of Irénée and Barbara du Pont's Granogue; Pierre and Elise du Pont's Patterns, and Frolic Weymouth's The Big Bend, to name just a few.

10. Pierre S. du Pont Papers, Series C, Hagley Museum & Library. Henry Algernon bought Eleutherian Mills for Louise Crowninshield; Pierre bought Nemours for the J. Simpson Deans, and Mary A. B. Laird bought Lower Louviers for her son Chick.

11. Karen Sisson Marshall, "The American Country House in the Greater Brandywine Valley: A Love Affair with the Land" (masters thesis, University of Delaware, 2002). Ferdinand Lundberg, *America's 60 Families* (New York: Vanguard, 1937), p. 420. R. L. Duffus, "Rulers of the Vast Empire of Du Pont," *The New York Times*, September 30, 1934.

12. Three generations of the Feliciani family have worked at Winterthur, for example. Ernest Dale and Charles Meloy, "Hamilton Macfarland Barksdale and the DuPont Contributions to Systematic Management," *Business History Review* 36, no. 2 (Summer 1962): 127–52. Chandler and Salsbury, *Pierre S. du Pont*, pp. xix–xxi, 594–600. William R. M. Binnie, "A History of Agriculture at Longwood Farms, 1906–1951" (masters thesis, University of Delaware, 1992), pp. 30–46. H. F. Davis, William Reed, and Mogens Plum, "Winterthur: A Study in Breeding Dairy Cattle," *Miscellaneous Publication 2* (November 1953), issued by the Agricultural Experiment Station, University of Nebraska.

13. Of the 60 houses examined in the chapters and Portfolio of this book, 24 were either constructed or had major additions between 1930 and 1940. American Institute of Architects files, Historical Society of Delaware.

14. A list of 70 would include those in this book, and the following: Doe Run, the 1937 estate owned by Esther du Pont and her husband, Sir John Thouron; Philip du Pont's ca. 1910 Fairville, PA estate; Fiskekill, the ca. 1935 estate owned by Edith du Pont and her husband, Richard Riegel; Foxcatcher, the 1920s William du Pont Jr. estate in Newtown Square, PA; L'Hermitage, a ca. 1930 estate owned by Victorine du Pont and her husband, Elbert Dent; Limestone Farm, later known as Carousel Farms, owned by A. Felix du Pont in the 1930s; Sophie du Pont and Ernest May's 1933 estate with a house designed by Walter Carlson; Rock Spring, the ca. 1930 estate owned by Irene Carpenter Kitchell with a house designed by Clarence R. Hope; Eleanor Frances du Pont and husband Philip Gordon Rust's ca. 1935 property of 116 acres on the Brandywine; Saint Amour Farm, Lammot du Pont's 8,000 acres in Pennsylvania; Phyllis Moxham du Pont and husband Porter Schutt's ca. 1935 estate with a house designed by Jim Thompson on the Rencourt property. Lundberg, *60 Families*.

15. For Okie, see Fair Hill chapter. From the late 1890s through 1918, Robeson Lea Perot, who married F. G. du Pont's daughter Eleanor in 1897, seemed to be the family's favorite architect. His commissions in Wilmington dried up after his ca. 1918 divorce from Eleanor. A partial list of other architects includes E. William Martin: Longwood, Dripping Spigots; Clarence R. Hope: Rock Spring, Brookdale Farm; Albert Ely Ives: Gibraltar, Chevannes, Winterthur, Calmar; Brown & Whiteside: Dilwyne Farms, Longwood, Old Nemours; DeArmand, Ashmead & Brinkley: Oberod, Gibraltar; Jim Thompson: Applecross and the Porter Schutt House. Thompson is best known for his revival of the Thai silk industry. Other residential work by Massena & du Pont includes the extended fountain garden at Nemours, the gatehouses and playhouse at Bellevue, a library addition at Saint Amour, and 1102 Hopeton Road. Bois-des-Fossés, now known as Brantwyn, serves as a wedding facility and conference center.

16. The firm is still in business, Homsey Architects, Inc., with the Homseys' son Eldon as one of the principals. Wilmington contractor John Bader built Bellevue and Gibraltar, while A. L. Lauritsen worked on Gibraltar, Winterthur, Chevannes, and Meown for Albert Ely Ives. American Car & Foundry went out of business in 1938, according to the American Institute of Architects files, Historical Society of Delaware. Wilmington Stair worked with H. F du Pont on his Winterthur Museum installations in the 1950s.

17. Marion Cran, *Gardens in America* (New York: Macmillan Company, 1932), p. 227. Coffin's office records indicate she also worked for Ernest du Pont at his house in town and for E. I. du Pont, Wilmington, in 1928.

ELEUTHERIAN MILLS

1. The family generally spells the name du Pont. The company spelling is DuPont. Peter Bauduy, a shareholder in the DuPont Company, drafted the plans and supervised the construction of Eleutherian Mills. Maureen O'Brien Quimby, *Eleutherian Mills*, rev. ed. (Wilmington, DE: Hagley Museum & Library, 1999), p. 13.

2. Thomas Coleman du Pont, Acc. 1503, Box 11, Hagley Museum & Library. Evelina du Pont championed the house in the 1890s and early 1900s, replacing glass when needed. When the property came up for sale in 1923, she encouraged Louise's ownership; see Recollections of Louise Crowninshield, 1958, "The Big Explosion," "Evelina du Pont," HF284, Winterthur Archives; see also Catherine Irving, oral history, Hagley Museum & Library.

3. In his account books, the Colonel began a special category, Old Homestead, to keep track of the costs incurred; HA Journal of Expenses, HA6, 7, 9, Winterthur Archives. Louise paid for alterations to the small building next to the house, called the Old Office, so that it could be used as a guesthouse; Louise Crowninshield to R. E. Ellis, January 24, 1928, LC Papers, B14, Winterthur Archives; see John Craig, HF 205, Winterthur Archives. See H. F. du Pont's letter to Louise Crowninshield, January 25, 1925, HF 541, Winterthur Archives. Mellor, Meigs & Howe had recently completed a house for Christopher Ward in nearby Centreville, DE; see Mellor, Meigs & Howe Papers, The Athenaeum of Philadelphia; and Pat Cannon, *Centreville: The History of a Delaware Village* (Centreville, DE: Centreville Civic Assoc., 2000), pp. 92–93. The story of the architect was told to the author by John Sweeney, who heard it from H. F. du Pont.

4. August 30, 1924, Acc. 471, Box 30, Hagley Museum & Library.

5. Evelina du Pont gave Louise some of the furniture that had been in the house before the explosion; see Recollections of Louise Crowninshield, "Evelina du Pont," HF284, Winterthur Archives. Ruth Lord, *H. F. du Pont and Winterthur: A Daughter's Portrait* (New Haven: Yale University Press, 1999), p. 149. Mrs. A. D. Irving, oral history, Hagley Museum & Library. Lord, *H. F. du Pont*, p. 147. Walt Biddle, oral history, p. 12, Hagley Museum & Library.

6. Walter Mellor to H. F. du Pont, January 19, 1924, HF541, Winterthur Archives.

7. Mac Griswold and Eleanor Weller, *The Golden Age of American Gardens* (New York: Abrams, 1991), p. 143. It is possible that the couple was influenced by the work of Frederick Crowninshield, Frank's uncle, who was a renowned painter of classical imagery and one of the founders of the American Academy in Rome. Almost no documentation survives telling us where Crowninshield purchased the late 19th- early 20th-century garden ornaments. Images of the garden at its height are available on the Smithsonian Archives of American Gardens Web site. Ruth's letter is in the Ruth Wales du Pont papers, Winterthur Archives.

LOWER LOUVIERS

1. Conversation with William "Mike" du Pont. Admiral Samuel Francis DuPont and his wife, Sophie, lived at Upper Louviers from 1839 until Sophie's death in 1888. The house, owned by A. I. duPont by 1903, was razed in 1978. The land is now part of the DuPont Country Club golf course.

2. For more on the du Pont family connection with Thomas Jefferson, see Dumas Malone, *Correspondence between Thomas Jefferson and Pierre Samuel du Pont de Nemours, 1798–1817* (Boston: Houghton Mifflin, 1930). Rosa is quoted in Mary Laird Silvia, *The Other Side of the River: A History of the Greater Louviers Property and Its Houses* (Privately printed, 2006). Many thanks to Mary Laird Silvia for her help.

3. There were two Hagley houses in close proximity. One survives today and is still a family home; the other was taken down in the 1940s.

OLD NEMOURS

1. Thomas Coleman du Pont, open letter to the family, April 8, 1914, Acc. 1503, Box 11, Hagley Museum & Library. In an attempt to avoid confusion on the part of the reader, the name Old Nemours is used throughout to distinguish this house from Nemours. The family, however, referred to both residences simply as Nemours.

2. Amy (Amelia) was a granddaughter of Victor du Pont, the daughter of Charles I. du Pont and his second wife, Ann Ridgely. Nemours is not far from Fontainebleau, about 60 miles south of Paris. In 1775 Pierre Samuel du Pont purchased a country house outside Nemours, near the village of Chevannes, and named it Bois-des-Fossés (Wood of the Trenches), a reference to nearby Roman ruins.

3. Eleutherian Mills and Lower Louviers were the other two near the mills. Alfred Victor's preferences are cited in Evelina du Pont Bidermann to her son, James, December 11, 1844, Acc. 761, Hagley Museum & Library.

4. "Alfred is building a little addition to his house, at the place where the blue piazza was, it is frame and will contain a school room and a pantry, Meta [Margaretta] intends converting her little parlor into a bedroom. I think this is a very good plan of enlarging the house at little expense & the way he has made it, it looks very pretty indeed" (Victorine du Pont Bauduy to Evelina du Pont Bidermann, August 28, 1838, Hagley Research File, Nemours, Hagley Museum & Library). Letters between Alfred Victor du Pont and Antoine Bidermann, 1837–41, Hagley Museum & Library. "Uncle Alfred's house is quite finished outside. It is plastered but the carpenters and painters are not done yet" (Evelina du Pont Bidermann to her son, August 9, 1844); "Your Uncle Alfred's house is entirely finished. It looks very well, particularly the staircase (you know his fondness for spiral staircases) and the little gallery in front of the gallery which has a view of the creek, the dam and Charles house and manufactory" (Evelina du Pont Bidermann to her son, December 11, 1844, Acc. 761, Hagley Museum & Library). Quote cited in Joseph Frazier Wall, *Alfred I. du Pont: The Man and His Family* (New York: Oxford University Press, 1990), p. 88; from E. Page Williamson to Mary P. Williamson, October 28, 1852, Acc. 1698, Hagley Museum & Library. For furnishings, see Emma Pauline du Pont's Book of Furniture, 1906–14, Acc. 1597, Box 3, Hagley Museum & Library. Certain items are noted as having been bought for the 1844 addition.

5. Alfred Victor's widow, Margaretta, moved to Goodstay.

6. Pierre Samuel du Pont, *Life in My Father's House*, ed. H. Rodney Sharp Jr. (Wilmington, DE: H. Rodney Sharp Jr., 1987).

7. Serious explosions at the mills occurred in 1847, 1857, and 1863. Repair work is documented for 1847, and an undated bill marked at a later date, probably 1856, is most likely 1857. Alfred Victor, a bibliophile, had bookcases built in 1845 and 1846. The kitchen yard was paved with bricks in 1853. For all these bills, see LMSS Group 4, Box 4 and 5, Hagley Museum & Library. The first floor measured 2,233 square feet; see 1900 Family Centennial Celebration, Acc. 761, Box 19, Hagley Museum & Library. Eugene was responsible for electrifying the company and the company houses after Henry's death. Memoirs of Richard Stout, 1909, oral history, Hagley Museum & Library.

8. Amy's mother was Ann Ridgely, the daughter of Henry Moore Ridgely. Ann Ridgely's stepmother, Sally Anne Comegys, lived at the family house on the Green in Dover, DE, until 1887. It is possible that she inherited the chairs at that time. Descendants of Eugene and Amy own some Ridgely chairs today. Other Ridgley pieces were later given to Henry Ridgley Jr. The 1894 photos, which include four of Ann's bedroom but none of the other family members, were made six months before Ann's wedding to Californian William Peyton and her subsequent relocation to Santa Cruz. Her maid of honor was Louise du Pont, later Crowninshield, who would one day occupy the house next door, Eleutherian Mills.

9. Note, 1979, Hagley Research File, Hagley Museum & Library.

10. Marion Cran, *Gardens in America* (New York: Macmillan Company, 1932), p. 227.

PELLEPORT

1. After Evelina's death in 1938, the portraits from the front parlor were scattered among the family. Today Hagley Museum & Library owns the one of Sophie; Winterthur owns those of Eleuthera and Victorine; and Evelina Bidermann's portrait is in France, in private hands. The three portraits from the dining room are now part of the Winterthur Museum collection. The wooden sheep and the bed are at Hagley Museum & Library.

SAINT AMOUR

1. Robeson Lea Perot made alterations to Rencourt in 1899; see *Philadelphia Real Estate Record and Builders' Guide* 14 (March 15, 1899): 161, n 11; and Philadelphia Architects and Buildings Web site, University of Pennsylvania and the Athenaeum of Philadelphia.

2. Alexis I. du Pont School, named after Francis G.'s father, is still an operating school on the site although it has been enlarged considerably.

3. Philadelphia Architects and Buildings Web site.

4. For Perot, see *Philadelphia Real Estate Record and Builders' Guide* 31 (October 4, 1916): 664, n 40; Philadelphia Architects and Buildings Web site, the Athenaeum of Philadelphia. For the ironwork, see Architectural Archives of the University of Pennsylvania, Samuel Yellin Collection, Job 2484, Philadelphia Architects and Buildings Web site, University of Pennsylvania and the Athenaeum of Philadelphia.

5. Maureen Quimby, "Country Houses along the Brandywine: The du Pont Legacy" (unpublished manuscript, 1991), Hagley Museum & Library.

6. Walter Carpenter's older brother R. R. M. Carpenter, married Margaretta du Pont, Mary Belin's youngest daughter. Interior designer Voruz de Vaux redid the interiors of the Square House; De Vaux to H. F. du Pont, February 5, 1924, HF 156, Winterthur Archives.

7. The little frame house was built in 1877 by Pierre Gentieu, a DuPont Company worker who enjoyed photography and took a great many photos of the Brandywine and du Pont family houses in the late 19th and early 20th centuries. Philadelphia Architects and Buildings Web site, University of Pennsylvania and the Athenaeum of Philadelphia.

808 BROOM STREET & OLD MILL

1. The Moors, in Horn Point, MD, was acquired about 1910. It had a ca. 1750 house that was destroyed by fire in 1948. The 60-acre Nevis property, with an 1830s house built by Alexander Hamilton's son, was donated to Columbia University in 1934; see *Nevis: Irvington-on-Hudson, New York* (New York: Columbia University, 1938).

2. He and Elsie were married in Wilmington in 1889. They spent their early married life in Central City, KY, and Johnstown, PA. Coleman was president of various coal and iron operations, from which he made a fortune.

3. The service spaces have not been recorded. The room names come from a ca. 1910–30 inventory book of 808 Broom Street, on microfilm at Hagley Museum & Library.

4. For a history of the farm and more about the house, see "The Old Mill, 1705–1929," a pamphlet written perhaps by a family member; and William Winder Laird, *The Old Mill* (Privately printed, 1973), both courtesy of Karen Farquhar. See also the correspondence of A. Bidermann du Pont, 1915–1921, at Hagley Museum & Library.

5. T. Coleman du Pont to Henry Francis du Pont, December 4, 1916, HF513, Winterthur Archives.

LONGWOOD

1. Dilks practiced architecture in the Philadelphia area between 1880 and 1917. He built Saint Amour, Pierre's mother's house. Brown & Whiteside worked on other Longwood buildings including the Webb barn and farm office and also on Nemours, for Pierre's niece Paulina Dean. The firm still exists as Moeckel Carbonell Associates, in Wilmington, Delaware.

2. The du Ponts also had a four-room suite in the Carleton House on Madison Avenue and 36th Street in New York City; an apartment in the Hotel Du Pont in Wilmington, which was primarily for Pierre; and a chateau in France that they shared with Alice's brother.

3. De Vaux had a shop in the DuPont Company office building in Wilmington as well as one at 635 Park Avenue in New York City. He remodeled Nemours in the 1930s when it was owned by P. S. du Pont's niece Paulina du Pont Dean. He provided French antiques to H. F. du Pont; worked on Rodney Sharp's house in Boca Grande and at Gibraltar; and was also hired by members of the Carpenter family.

NEMOURS

1. Alicia gave up the apartment at 43 Avenue du Bois de Boulogne in 1916.

2. Marquis James, *Alfred I. duPont: The Family Rebel* (Indianapolis: Bobbs-Merrill, 1941), p. 465. A. I. duPont, "A Few Notes," May 15, 1914, Box 53, File 12–13, Washington & Lee University.

3. In 1917 Brentano's published her translation of a book of 17th-century French poetry, *Ode of Fénelon*.

GIBRALTAR

1. Delaware College is now the University of Delaware. Iris Gestram, "The Historic Landscape at Gibraltar: A Proposal for Its Preservation" (masters thesis, University of Delaware, 1997), pp. 24–25. H. Rodney Sharp oral history, *Wilmington News Journal*, 1960s, Winterthur Archives.

2. As quoted in Robert L. Raley, *H. Rodney Sharp, 1880–1968: Biographical Notes* (Winterthur, DE: Henry Francis du Pont Winterthur Museum, 1980), n.p. Thelma Humphries Sharp oral history, 1989, Winterthur Archives.

3. For the firm, see *Philadelphia Real Estate Record and Builder's Guide* 29, no. 21 (May 27, 1914): 337. Philadelphia Architects and Buildings Web site, University of Pennsylvania and the Philadelphia Athenaeum. In 1924 they worked on the R. R. M. Carpenter residence with interior designer Oscar Mertz. In 1935–37, they designed the Jane du Pont and Harry Lunger House, Oberod. They also designed Sharp's cabin on the Eastern Shore. Gestram, "Historic Landscape at Gibraltar," p. 26. Bader was the builder at Bellevue as well. In reference to Chevannes, Sharp wrote to Albert Ely Ives that he disliked a house of "the ordinary type of going into a front hall and seeing rooms on either side of the front door" (July 19, 1926, P. S. du Pont files, Hagley Museum & Library). His mother was the Baronne Voruz de Vaux of Chateau de la Houssaye, a

descendant of Alexandre Charles, Duke of Lorraine.

4. Architectural Archives of the University of Pennsylvania, Samuel Yellin Collection, no. 49.1919 and 49.1032, Philadelphia Architects and Builders Web site, University of Pennsylvania and the Athenaeum of Philadelphia.

5. During Ives's short career in Wilmington (he left in 1935), he also built a retreat for Isabella that she called Meown Farm. H. Rodney Sharp to H. F. du Pont, July 29, 1927, HF600, Winterthur Archives. Jeffrey Hamilton, Rebecca Siders, Kelli Dobbs, and Amy Richards, "Gibraltar: The H. Rodney Sharp House, Wilmington, Delaware: An Architectural Description and Photographic Documentation of Four Major Rooms" (typescript, 1999, Center for Historic Architecture and Design, University of Delaware, Newark), p. 2.

6. He would later sell antiques to the Lammot du Pont Copelands at Mt. Cuba.

7. In 1958 he gave the Corbit house to Winterthur, followed by the Brick Hotel in 1966. The houses have been returned to the town of Odessa and the Historic Odessa Foundation. In addition to being a major figure in the preservation community of Delaware, Sharp is probably best known as significant force in the reshaping of Delaware College into the University of Delaware. The university requested that Sharp make a list of his major interests in 1966 for its permanent files; Gestram, "Historic Landscape at Gibraltar," p. 14, Sharp Files, Historic Houses of Odessa.

OWL'S NEST

1. For more on Owl's Nest, see Barksdale Maynard, *Buildings of Delaware* (Charlottesville: University of Virginia Press, 2008). Shipman worked on at least two other du Pont family houses in this period, including Ernest du Pont, whose 1925 Spanish-style house was designed by William Woodburn Potter. H. F. du Pont employed Louise Edey at Winterthur in 1928 and at his Southampton house, Chestertown, in 1924–25.

2. These details help identify the former estate buildings in the housing developments that now surround the property.

3. See Lewis Colt Albro and Harrie T. Lindeberg, *Domestic Architecture* (Cambridge: Privately printed, 1912).

4. The previous work was for Philip B. Jennings, Bennington, VT, 1915; and Mrs. Frederick G. Achelis, Greenwich, CT, 1919. See Judith Tankard, *The Gardens of Ellen Biddle Shipman* (Sagaponeck, NY: Sagapress in association with the Library of American Landscape History, 1996), p. 54, 207 n 9.

SECOND OFFICE

1. The stone was the locally quarried Brandywine granite, a form of gneiss.

2. The recollection was related to the author by Jean's grandson Everitt du Pont. Perot and Eleanor Ball du Pont, Paul's sister, divorced in 1919.

GRANOGUE

1. Henry Algernon du Pont, owner of the Wilmington & Northern Rail line, changed the name of the Smith Bridge rail station to Granogue, a word said to be a place name in France with significance to the family. The history has not been traced.

2. The core of this collection was purchased in 1920 from Dr. George F. Kunz, the gemologist at Tiffany's. The collection was subsequently donated to the University of Delaware.

3. The family's former residence, now the site of the Tower Hill School field house, was near Saint Amour.

4. Irénée du Pont Jr., *The New House at Granogue* (unpublished memoir, 2007), chap. 3.

CHEVANNES

1. Ives to Rodney Sharp, April 1, 1927, P. S. du Pont Papers, Box 783, Series A, Hagley Museum & Library.

WINTERTHUR

1. On "paintings," see reference to seamstress Miss S. M. du Beust, January 28, 1927, HF286, Winterthur Archives. Louise Edey, a New York interior designer, who also worked at Owl's Nest, supervised the 1927 painting, wallpapering, and reupholstering. Anna Butler's quote was recounted by her daughter, oral history, Winterthur Archives

2. John. R. Schoemer, Winterthur Archives.

3. On the layoffs, see H. F. du Pont to Bert Ives, October 19, 1938, Winterthur Archives. John R. Schoemer, Winterthur Archives.

GARDEN CLUB OF AMERICA

1. Letter to Louis Lelieur, quoted in Norman B. Wilkinson, *E. I. du Pont, Botaniste: The Beginning of a Tradition* (Charlottesville: University of Virginia Press, 1972), p. 49.

NOTES

APPLECROSS

1. Wilhelmina Ross, a former president of the Garden Club of America, donated Applecross material to that organization. She listed the original architect of the house as James Thompson, with Victorine and Samuel Homsey the architects of a later addition. Thompson, who was trained as an architect and practiced until 1940, is best known for his postwar work with the Thai silk industry and his mysterious disappearance in 1967. Thompson and Wilhelmina du Pont grew up together and were friends, according to Wilhelmina's daughter Joan Bolling (conversation with author, June 27, 2008).

2. *Country Life in America* (August 1929). Chamberlin developed the Schwab estate in Loretto, PA; Colonel Robert H. Montgomery's garden in Greenwich, CT; and was the consulting landscape architect for Montgomery's Fairchild Tropical Gardens in Miami. H. F. du Pont was a director of Fairchild Tropical Gardens and wrote: "The Montgomerys have, I imagine, the most beautifully planted palm landscaping in the world & the Fairchild Gardens are full of interest" (March 27, 1948, HF313, Winterthur Archives). Interview with Richard W. Lighty, December 1993, cited in Elizabeth Varley, "The du Pont Family Legacy of Horticulture in the Brandywine Valley" (master's thesis, University of Delaware, 1995).

3. The Rosses had a summer place, Land's End, in Saranac Lake, NY; shooting plantations in Rock Hall, MD and Guerrytown, AL; and a 1,000-acre farm, Renappi, in nearby Hockessin, DE.

FAIR HILL

1. Rencourt, Saint Amour, Pelleport, and the 1902 Winterthur can be cited as appealing to the older generation.

2. The house, completed in 1927, was named Squirrel Run after a local creek. S. Hallock married Elizabeth Ormond Wrenn on June 12, 1926. Esther Driver du Pont married Campbell Weir on September 15, 1928.

BELLEVUE

1. In 1893 William Sr. bought Woolton Hall, a Gothic Revival house with castellated towers built by Hanson Robinson. William renamed the property Bellevue and trained carriage and draft horses on the property; see C. C. Furtz appraisal, January 29, 1928, Hagley Museum & Library, courtesy of Tanya Brun.

2. According to his obituary (*The New York Times*, January 1, 1966), he designed more than 25 horse racing courses. Massena & du Pont's blueprints are in the Bader Papers, Acc. 407, Hagley Museum & Library.

3. The 1943 National Women's Indoor Tennis Championships were held here.

MT. CUBA

1. Valencia Libby, oral history, early 1980s, Winterthur Archives.

2. H. F. du Pont to Lammot Copeland, June 29, 1935, HF281, Winterthur Archives. American Car & Foundry also did work for H. F. du Pont and Irénée du Pont at Granogue. John W. Cornell Jr., *History of a Philadelphia Builder* (1975), p. 24.

3. The name Andelot refers to the area in France where the Belin family originates.

OBEROD

1. Philip is probably best known as the primary complainant in the 1916 lawsuit against Pierre du Pont. Except for the first, *Under the Blue Sky* (Philadelphia: G. W. Jacobs, ca. 1900), all his books of poetry were published by Patterson & White of Philadelphia: *Currente calemo* (1907); *New Poems and a Play* (1914); *Oberod and Other Poems* (1919).

2. The firm remodeled Gibraltar and worked on Dilwyne.

3. The whitewash was removed early on.

4. H. F. du Pont sold her some French antiques as he developed his American collection; Letter, Lunger Papers, January 8, 1938, courtesy of the Jones family.

THE COTTAGE AT WINTERTHUR

1. They gave up the apartment at 280 Park Avenue because of concerns about the war and later used their daughter's apartment at 635 Park Avenue as a *pied-à-terre*.

BIBLIOGRAPHY

GENERAL

Cannon, Pat. *Centreville: The History of a Delaware Village*. Centreville, Delaware: Centreville Civic Association, 2002.

Chandler, Alfred D. Jr., and Stephen Salsbury. *Pierre S. du Pont and the Making of the Modern Corporation*. New York: Harper and Row, 1971.

Cran, Marion. *Gardens in America*. New York: Macmillan Company, 1932.

Griswold, Mac, and Eleanor Weller. *The Golden Age of American Gardens*. New York: Abrams, 1991.

Henry, Allan J. *Francis Guerney du Pont: A Memoir*. Philadelphia: William F. Fell Co., 1951.

———. *The Life of Alexis I. du Pont*. Philadelphia: William F. Fell Co., 1945.

Lauritsen Construction Brochure, ca. 1935. Hagley Museum & Library.

Lundberg, Ferdinand. *America's 60 Families*. New York: Vanguard, 1937.

Marshall, Karen. "The American Country House in the Greater Brandywine Valley: A Love Affair with the Land." Master's thesis, University of Delaware, 2002.

Maynard, Barksdale. *Buildings of Delaware*. Charlottesville: University of Virginia Press, 2008.

Tankard, Judith B. *The Gardens of Ellen Shipman*. New York: Sagaponack Press, 1996.

ELEUTHERIAN MILLS

Quimby, Maureen O'Brien. *Eleutherian Mills*. Wilmington, Delaware: Hagley Museum & Library, 1999.

ELTON

Landscape Architecture Quarterly (April 1938).

Rehman, Elsa. *Garden Making*. Boston: Houghton Mifflin, 1926.

GIBRALTAR

Elwood, P. H., Jr. *American Landscape Architecture*. New York: Architectural Book Publishing Co., 1924.

LOUVIERS

Eldrick, Elise du Pont. "Louviers: Upper House." Unpublished transcript, 1970. Winterthur Archives.

Silvia, Mary Laird. *The Other Side of the River: A History of the Greater Louviers Property and Its Houses*. Privately printed, 2006.

MEOWN

"The Playhouse That Grew to Full Size." *House & Garden* (May 1951).

NEMOURS

"Alfred I. du Pont's Estate Nemours." *The Spur* (May 15, 1914).

Aslet, Clive. *The American Country House*. New Haven: Yale University Press, 1990.

"The Country Seat of Mr. Alfred du Pont." *Town & Country* (June 28, 1913).

Hewitt, Mark Alan, Kate Lemos, William Morrison, and Charles Warren. *Carrère & Hastings Architects*. New York: Acanthus Press, 2006.

House & Garden's Second Book of Gardens (1927).

"House for Alfred I. du Pont, Esq. Wilmington, Del." *American Architect* (August 31, 1910).

James, Marquis. *Alfred I. du Pont: The Family Rebel*. Indianapolis: Bobbs-Merrill, 1941.

"A Palatial Country House in Delaware: The A. I. du Pont Residence." *Architectural Record* (October 1913).

Town & Country (January 15, 1932).

Wall, Joseph Frazier. *Alfred I. du Pont: The Man and His Family*. New York: Oxford University Press, 1990.

OLD NEMOURS

"The Gardens of Mr. and Mrs. J. Simpson Dean, Wilmington, Delaware." *Country Life* (August 1929).

OWL'S NEST

Albro, Lewis Colt, and Harrie T. Lindeberg. *Domestic Architecture*. Cambridge: Privately printed, 1912.

Arts & Decoration (November 1922).

Domestic Architecture of H. T. Lindeberg. New York: Acanthus Press, 1996.

Price, C. Matlock. "A Note of Quiet Distinction in Country House Interiors: Some Recent Work of Harris [sic] T. Lindeberg of the Former Firm Albro and Lindeberg." *Arts & Decoration* (October 1914).

"Residence of Eugene du Pont, Greenville, Del." *Arts & Decoration* (January 20, 1920).

SAINT AMOUR

Cane, Percy. "Modern Gardens: British and Foreign." *The Studio* (1926–27).

TULIP HOLLOW

"Built-in Features." *Architectural Forum* (October 1941).

"House in Hockessin, Delaware." *Architectural Forum* (June 1944).

"Open House in the Suburbs." *House & Garden* (February 1946).

"Portfolio of Recent Work by Victorine and Samuel Homsey, Wilmington, Delaware." *Architectural Forum* (September 1940).

"A Thousand Women in Architecture" (Victorine Homsey). *Architectural Record* (June 1948).

WINTERTHUR

Cantor, Jay. *Winterthur*. New York: Abrams, 1985.

Du Pont, H. F. "The Development of a Country Place, 1897–1902." Unpublished transcript, 1902. Winterthur Archives.

Lord, Ruth. *H. F. du Pont and Winterthur: A Daughter's Portrait*. New Haven: Yale University Press, 1999.

Magnani, Denise. *The Winterthur Garden: Henry Francis du Pont's Romance with the Land*. New York: Abrams, 1995.

Sweeney, John A. H. "The Winterthur Residence of Mr. and Mrs. Henry Francis du Pont." *The Magazine Antiques* (May 1964).

INDEX

Page numbers in *italics* refer to illustrations

Addison Mizner architects, 98, 132, 135
Alfred I. duPont Hospital for Children, 90
Alfred I. duPont Testamentary Trust, 90
Allen & Collens architects, 188
American Architect, 86
American Car & Foundry, 23, 176
American Horticultural Society, 23
American Institute of Architects (AIA), 21, 65
Andelot farm, 179
Anderson, Josephine (Mrs. Victor du Pont Jr.), 207
Antiques, 16–17, 48, 98, 132, 134–35, 163, 177, 186
Applecross house, 23
Archibald M. L. du Pont House, 207
Architects, 22. *See also* individual names
Architectural Forum, 189
Architectural Record, 86, 204
Arthurs, Stanley, 119, *121*
Austin, Jean (Mrs. William du Pont Jr.), 167–68
Automobile age, 116–17. *See also* General Motors

Bach, Oscar, 102, 104
Bader, John A., 96, 167
Ball, Jessie (Mrs. Alfred I. duPont), 88, 90
Barber, Joel, 207
Bayard, Thomas Francis, 206
Beaux-Arts landscape, 98–99, 134
Belin, Alice (Mrs. Pierre Samuel du Pont), 78–79, 82
Belin, Louisa (Mrs. John P. Wales), 204
Belin, Mary (Mrs. Lammot du Pont), 46, 58–59, 61, 63–64, 150, 202
Bellevue house, 18, 24
Berberyan, Ohan, 99
Bidermann, Antoine, 195
Bidermann Country Club, 207
Bidermann, Mrs. Antoine. *See* du Pont, Evelina
Bie, Maria Alexia du Pont Ortiz de, 206
Big Bend house, The, *24*, 25
Bissell & Perot architects, 204–05
Bois-des-Fossé house (France), 14, *15*, 17, *119*, 120

Bois-des-Fossé house (Wilmington, DE), 22, *211*
Bois-des-Fossés (Arthurs), 119, *121*
Boxwood, 123–28
Bradford, Elizabeth Canby, 205
Bradford, Mary Alicia (Mrs. George Amory Maddox). *See* du Pont, Alicia
Brandywine Conservancy, 24
Brandywine Garden Club, 111
Brandywine granite, 59, 96, 204–05
Brandywine River Museum, 25
Brandywine River School of painters, 25
Breck, William, 203
Brickbuilider, 206
Brinton, Josephine (Mrs. Ernest du Pont), 65
Brookdale Farm house, 23, 206
Broom, Jacob, 203
Broom Street house, 69, *70*, *71*, *72*, *74*
Brown & Whiteside architects, 22, 77, 208
Buck, C. Douglass, 161, 203, 207
Buck, Mrs. C. Douglass. *See* du Pont, Alice
Buena Vista house, 19, 21, 161, 164, 207, 208
Building materials, 34, 73–74, 96, 113, 156, 160, 176, 197
Butler, Anna, 132

Calmar house, *209*
Campbell, John, 61
Carillon tower, *20*, *21*, 22, 90
Carpenter, Louisa d'Andelot (Mrs. John King Jenney), 208–09
Carpenter, R. R. M., Jr., 23, 26, 211
Carpenter, Robert Ruliph Morgan, 208
Carpenter, Walter S., 67
Carpenter, Walter S., III, 206
Carpenter, Walter S., Jr., 206
Carrère & Hastings architects, 16, 22, 85, 86, 90
Carrère, John. *See* Carrère & Hastings architects
Chamberlin, Noel, 23, 51, 149, 211
Chandler, Theophilus Parsons, 15, *52*, 53, *57*, 59, *62*, 204–05
Chapel at Big Bend house, 25
Charles Schwab estate, 23
Chateau Country (Delaware), 13, 18
Chicago World's Columbian Exposition, 79

INDEX

Chichester, Mary (Mrs. A. Felix du Pont), 65, 67, 142
Chippendale furniture, 177
Classical style, 37
Clayton, John, 207
Coffin, Marian Cruger, 23, 63, 94, 97–99, 132, 134, 142, *144*, *145*, *150*, *152*, 179, 201
Coleman du Pont Homsey (Hurd), *189*
Colonial Revival style, 34, 161
    architecture, 55, 63, 98, 110, 149–50, 160, 165, 176, 186, 205
    gardens, 48, 164–65, 177, 204
Colonial Williamsburg, 176, 200
Communal property system, 13
Conservatories, 22, 46, 55, 72, 77, 83, 88, 98, 113, 135, 198, 203–05
Converse, Bernard T., 167
Cope, J. Walter, 79
Copeland, Charles, 63–64
Copeland house, *62*, 63
Copeland, Lammot du Pont, 23, 26, 175–77
Copeland, Mrs. Charles Copeland. *See* du Pont, Louisa
Copeland, Mrs. Lammot du Pont. *See* Cunningham, Pamela
Cornelius, Charles O., 132
Cotswold style, 22
Country houses, *12*, 14–15, 18, 21–22, 24. *See also* individual names
Country Life, 142
Coverdale farm, 173–74
Craig, Mary, 210
Cran, Marion, 23, 208
Crawford Greenewalt House, *209*
Crooked Billet house, *205*
Crowninshield, Francis B., *22*, 34, 36, *37*
Crowninshield, Mrs. Francis B. *See* du Pont, Louise
Cunningham, Pamela (Mrs. Lammot du Pont Copeland), 13, 175–79

Dalmas, Charles, 202
Dauneport house, *210*
Davis, F. B., Jr., 124
Dean, J. Simpson, 23, 51
Dean, Mrs. J. Simpson. *See* du Pont, Paulina
DeArmand, Ashmead & Bickley architects, 22, 96, 183
Delaware Nature Society, 174
Dilks, Albert, 59, *61*, 63–64, 68, 77
Dilwyne Farms house, 18, *208*
Doggone house, *210*
Dogwood house, *11*, 208
Donaldson, John, 72
Downs, Ellason, 210
Downs, Robert Norton, III, 211
Dripping Spigots house, 18, *170*, *174*
du Pont, A. Bidermann, 206
du Pont, A. Felix, *26*, 65, 67, 205
du Pont, Alexis I., 110, 202, 205, 210
du Pont, Alfred Victor, *22*, *26*, 45, 46, 47, 63, 88, 90, 202, 209
du Pont, Alice Eugenie (Mrs. Julien de Villiers Ortiz), 206
du Pont, Alice (Mrs. C. Douglass Buck), 161, 164, 203, 207
du Pont, Alice (Mrs. Thomas Coleman du Pont), 70, 72–74, 77
du Pont, Alicia (Mrs. George Amory Maddox/Mrs. Alfred I. duPont), 85, 202

du Pont, Amy (Mrs. Eugene du Pont), 45–48, 51, 55, 57, 210
du Pont, Ann Ridgely, 48, 50
du Pont, Archibald M. L., 207
du Pont, Bella. *See* du Pont, Isabella
du Pont, Bessie G. (Mrs. Alfred I. duPont), 118–22, 204
du Pont, Charles I., 47
du Pont, Charles I., Jr., 203
du Pont, Charlotte (Mrs. Eleuthère Irénée II), 204
du Pont, Coleman. *See* du Pont, Thomas Coleman
du Pont, Dulcinea Ophelia Payne (Mrs. George Tyler Weymouth), 208, 210
du Pont, E. Frances (Mrs. Richard Morgan), 158, 160–61, 163, 165
du Pont, E. Paul, 107–08, 110–11, 203
du Pont, Eleuthère Irénée, 13–14, *26*, 28–29, 39, 45–46, 55, 78, 113, 141, 202–03
du Pont, Eleuthère Irénée, II, 204
du Pont, Elizabeth Bradford, 206
du Pont, Elizabeth Murton (Mrs. Walter S. Carpenter III), 206
du Pont, Ellen (Mrs. Robert Wheelwright/Mrs. Hollyday Meeds), 74, 204
du Pont, Elsie, 15
du Pont, Emily Tybout, 210
du Pont, Emma Pauline, 204
du Pont, Ernest, 65
du Pont, Esther (Mrs. Campbell Weir), 160, 164
du Pont, Ethel Hallock (Mrs. William K. du Pont), 51, 67, 68, 142, 150
du Pont, Ethel (Mrs. Franklin Delano Roosevelt Jr.), *102*
du Pont, Eugene E., *11*, *26*, 103, 208
du Pont, Eugene, III, 210
du Pont, Eugene, Jr., 100, 102–04, 106
du Pont, Eugene, Sr., *26*, 32, 44–48, 51, 55, 176
du Pont, Evelina, 32, 52–53, 55, 56, 119, 205
du Pont, Evelina (Mrs. Antoine Bidermann), 195, 202
du Pont family
    architecture preferred by, 14, 188
    centennial celebration of, 45, 61
    country houses owned by, *12*, 22
    French origins of, 13–14, 45, 85, 119
    gardens of, 141–42
    horticultural reputation of, 23
    philanthropy and, 24, 99
    shared values of, 24
    vacation homes and, 22
    wealth of, 14–16, 21–22, 24
du Pont, Francis G., 62, 203, 205–06
du Pont, Francis I., 202
du Pont, Gabrielle Josephine (Mrs. William Breck), 203
du Pont, Harry. *See* du Pont, Henry Francis
du Pont, Henry, 13, *26*, 32, 108
du Pont, Henry Algernon, 14–15, 32, 34–35, 132, 149, 195, 208
du Pont, Henry Belin, *26*, 38, 202–03, 210
du Pont, Henry Belin, Jr., 39, 161
du Pont, Henry Francis, *17*, *26*, 34, 97–99, 122, 129, 132, 139, 142, 149, 156, 176, 194–95, 197–201, 208
du Pont, Irene (Mrs. Irénée du Pont), 67, 117
du Pont, Irene S., 203
du Pont, Irénée, *26*, 46, 67, 112–13, 116–17

INDEX

du Pont, Isabella (Mrs. H. Rodney Sharp), 92–93, 96, 142, 154, *155*, 156
du Pont, Jane (Mrs. Harry W. Lunger), 182–83, 186
du Pont, Jean Ellen, 205
du Pont, Jean Kane Foulke (Mrs. E. Paul du Pont), 108, 110, *111*, 203
du Pont, Lammot, 17, *26*, 46, 59, 63, 142, 160
du Pont, Lammot, Jr., 183
du Pont, Louisa Gerhard (Mrs. Henry du Pont), 32, 47, 52–53, 56
du Pont, Louisa (Mrs. Charles Copeland), 63–64, 142, 176
du Pont, Louise (Mrs. Francis B. Crowninshield), 34, 36–37
du Pont, Lydia, 205–06
du Pont, Margaretta Lammot (Mrs. Robert R. M. Carpenter), 208
du Pont, Margaretta (Mrs. Alfred V. du Pont), 59, 204
du Pont, Margaretta (Mrs. Crawford H. Greenewalt), 170–74, 209
du Pont, Mariana, 203
du Pont, Marion, 167, *169*
du Pont, Mary Alletta Belin (Mrs. William W. Laird), 39, 41, 64, 203, 210–11
du Pont, Mary Pauline Foster, 15
du Pont, Mary Sophie (Mrs. Charles I. du Pont Jr.), 203
du Pont, Mary Van Dyke, 203
du Pont, May Lammot (Mrs. William du Pont), 53
du Pont, Mina. *See* du Pont, Wilhelmina (Mrs. Donald Ross)
Du Pont Motors, *110*, *111*
du Pont, Mrs. A. Felix. *See* Chichester, Mary
du Pont, Mrs. Alfred Victor. *See* Lammot, Margaretta
du Pont, Mrs. Charles I. *See* Ridgely, Ann
du Pont, Mrs. E. Paul. *See* du Pont, Jean Kane Foulke
du Pont, Mrs. Ernest. *See* Brinton, Josephine and Thompson, Anne
du Pont, Mrs. Eugene. *See* du Pont, Amy
du Pont, Mrs. Eugene, Jr. *See* Pyle, Ethel
du Pont, Mrs. Henry Belin. *See* Lewis, Margaret Wilson
du Pont, Mrs. Henry Francis. *See* du Pont, Ruth
du Pont, Mrs. Irénée. *See* du Pont, Irene
du Pont, Mrs. Lammot. *See* Belin, Mary
du Pont, Mrs. Nicholas. *See* Estes, Genevieve
du Pont, Mrs. Pierre Samuel. *See* Belin, Alice
du Pont, Mrs. Thomas Coleman. *See* du Pont, Alice
du Pont, Mrs. William. *See* du Pont, May Lammot
du Pont, Mrs. William, Jr. *See* Austin, Jean and Osborne, Margaret
du Pont, Mrs. William K. *See* du Pont, Ethel Hallock
du Pont, Natalie (Mrs. George P. Edmonds), 123–24, 126
du Pont, Nicholas, 161, 211
du Pont, Paulina (Mrs. J. Simpson Dean), 51, 97, 142, 149
du Pont, Phyllis Moxham (Mrs. Charles Porter Schutt), 208
du Pont, Pierre Samuel, 13, 16–18, 24, *26*, 46, 51, 59, 61, 68, 72, 75–81, 86, 93, 97, 119, 121, 142, 204, 207
du Pont, Pierre Samuel, III, 22, 211
du Pont, Ruth (Mrs. Henry Francis du Pont), 37, 135, 139, 199–201
du Pont, S. Hallock, 160, 209
du Pont, Sophie Madeline (Mrs. Samuel Francis DuPont), 46, 202
du Pont, Sophie (Mrs. Theophilus Parsons Chandler), 15, *57*
du Pont, Thomas Coleman, 16, 69–70, 72–74, 76, 86, 203–04, 206–07
du Pont, Victor, 39, 53
du Pont, Victor, Jr., 207
du Pont, Victorine (Mrs. A. Lentilhon Foster), 204

du Pont, Victorine (Mrs. Samuel Homsey), *19*, 22–23, 55, 57, 150, 156, 176, 187–89
du Pont, Wilhelmina (Mrs. Donald Peabody Ross), 148–50, *153*
du Pont, William, *26*, 53, 167, 205
du Pont, William, Jr., 124, 166–69, 205
du Pont, William K., 51, 108
duPont, Alfred I., 16–17, 20–21, 24, 72, 76, 84–86, 119, 202–04
DuPont Company, 17, 21, 29, 93, 108, 110, 207
  board of directors, 26, 76
  gunpowder explosions and, 46–47, 53, 202–03
  gunpowder mills of, 13–14, *16*, 17, 32, 36, 39, 45
  houses owned by, 32, 149, 202–05, 207–08, 211
  presidents of, 17, 45–47, 67, 70, 113, 117, 173, 206
  stock of, 102–03
DuPont Country Club, 202, 211
DuPont Engineering Company, 79
DuPont Highway, 70, *74*
duPont, Mrs. Alfred I. *See* du Pont, Bessie G. and du Pont, Alicia and Ball, Jessie
DuPont, Samuel Francis, 55, 202
Durham, Walter K., 65

E. F. Hodgson Company, 171
Early American style, 134
Edey, Louise, 102
Edmonds, George P., 123–24, 126
Edmonds, Mrs. George P. *See* du Pont, Natalie
Eldon du Pont Homsey (Hurd), *188*
Electric lighting, 47, 73, 203
Eleutherian Mills and Mill Buildings (Neuville), *14*
Eleutherian Mills house, 14–15, 17, 22, 24, 47, 53, 108, 141
Elrick, Elise du Pont, 202
Elton house, 65, 66, 67, 142, *144*
Empire style, 121
English style, 104, 124, 126, *127*, 199
Ernest du Pont house, 65
Estes, Genevieve (Mrs. Nicholas du Pont), 211

Fair Hill house, 23, 186
Farms, 13, 18, 21, 48, 61, 75–76, 79, 102–03, 106, 117, 132, 139, 149, 156, 160, 168, 173–74, 205, 208
Farquhar, Donald, 203
Farquhar, Dorcas Van Dyke (Mrs. Donald Farquhar), 203
Federal style, 35–36, 186, 208
Finch, Dr. and Mrs. Ronald, 209
Floor plans, *30*, *43*, *82*, *90*, *106*, *109*, *122*, *128*, *165*, *167*, *180*, *186*, *193*, *201*
Foster, A. Lentilhon, 204
Fouilhoux, J. Andre, 207
Foxcatcher Farm, 167–68
Frank and Louise du Pont Crowninshield (Molas), *29*
French style
  architecture, 85, 119–20, 156, 186, 208–09
  furnishings, 88, 120–21, 186
  gardens, 85–86, *87*, 120
G. W. McCauley & Son builders, 210
Garden Club of America, 23, 67, 140–42, 211
Garden Club of Wilmington, 141–42, 189

INDEX

Gardens
  Beaux Arts, 98–99, 134
  boxwood, 42, 102, 124, *145*, 164
  classical, *33*, *34*, 37, 142
  Colonial Revival, 48
  flower, 36, *75*, 104, 106, 164, 186
  formal, 63, 85–86, 111, 179
  fountain, 17, 76, 79, 98, 106, 142, 149
  French style, 85–86, 87, 120
  naturalistic, 36–37, 74, 117, 139, 179, 204
  parterre, 104, 117, 141
  production, 62, 111
  rock, *117*, 179
  sundial, *140*, *146*
  terraced, 97–98, 102, 124, 142, 149, 164, 208
  water lily, 66, *105*
  See also individual houses
Gardens in America (Cran), 23, 208
General Motors, 17, 76, 116
Georgian style, 72, 78, 113, 124, 161, 211
Gibralter house, 23, 141–42, *144*
Gilchrist, Edmond, 204
Godley, Frederick, 207
Golden Age of American Gardens, The (Weller and Griswold), 37
Golf courses, *75*, 79, 134, 139
Good Roads Movement, 70
Goodstay farm, 61–62
Goodstay house, 24, 59, 141, *204*
Gothic Revival, 167
Grace, Eugene, 195, 197
Granogue house, 18, 160
Great Depression, 21, 79, 134, 139, 176, 188
Greek-Revival style, 46–47, 202
Greenewalt, Crawford H., *26*, 170–74, 209
Greenewalt, Mrs. Crawford H. *See* du Pont, Margaretta
Greenville Country Club, 106
Griswold, Mac, 37

H. B. Du Pont House, *210*
Hagley Foundation, 203
Hagley House, 14–15, *202*, 203
Hagley (Jacob Broom) House, 203
Hagley Museum & Library, 24, 209
Hardware, 132, 164, 199
Harper, Alexander, 79
Hastings, Thomas, 85, 90. *See also* Carrère & Hastings architects
Hayward, Elizabeth (Mrs. Archibald du Pont), 207
Heatherley, Bernard, 183, *184*
Herter Brothers, 210
Hirons, John, 203
Historic preservation, 47, 93, 200
Historical styles, 22, 41–42, 121–22, 135, 163, 188, 197
Hodgson, Ernest Franklin, 171
Hodgson prefab houses, 170–71, *173*
Holcomb, Frederick, 211
Holcomb, Jane (Mrs. Pierre Samuel du Pont III), 211
Holden McLaughlin architects, 22

Homsey Architects, *19*, 22–23, 64, 67, *153*, *156*, 186, 203, 206–07, 209–10. *See also* Homsey, Samuel Eldon and du Pont, Victorine
Homsey, Mrs. Samuel. *See* du Pont, Victorine
Homsey, Samuel Eldon, *19*, 22–23, 150, 156, 176, 187–89
Hood, Raymond, 207
Hope, Clarence R., 22, 206
Horticultural Society of New York, 142
Horticulture, 23, 61, 68, 77, 98, 141–42
Horticulture, 142
Hotel Du Pont, *207*
House & Garden, 102, 171
Humphries, Elmer, 204
Hurd, Henriette Wyeth, 188–89
Hyde, J. A. Lloyd, 99

Indian Motorcycle Company, 111
Indian Springs Farm, 176
Interior decorators, 51, 99, 102. *See also* individual names
International Style, 176, 188
Irving, Catherine, 36
Irving, Evelyn, 204
Ives, Albert Ely, 22, 68, 98, *118*, 119–22, *131*, 132, 134–35, 156, 171, 209

J. S. Cornell & Son builders, 23, 176, 204
Jacobean-Norman style, 34
Jefferson, Thomas, 39, 55
Johnson, Walter J., 186

Kane, Margaret, 17
Keen, Charles Barton, 206
Kelsey, Seth, 179
Kruse, Albert, 203

Lafayette, Marquis de, 39, 55, 56
Laird, Alletta d'Andelot (Mrs. Robert Norton Downs III), 211
Laird, Chick. *See* Laird, William Winder, Jr.
Laird, Mary (Mrs. Ellason Downs), 210
Laird, Mrs. William Winder, Jr. *See* Moreton, Winnifred
Laird, Mrs. William W. *See* du Pont, Mary Alletta Belin
Laird, Rosa, 41
Laird, William Winder, Jr., 38–39, 41–42, 203
Laird, William W., 64
Lammot, Margaretta (Mrs. Alfred Victor du Pont), 45
Landscape architects, 23, 51, 102, 141. *See also* individual names
Landscape Architecture, 204
Lauritsen, A. L., 98, 122, 156, 209–10
Letdown house, *211*
Lewis & Valentine landscapers, 63, 97, 120, *185*, 186, 207, 211
Lewis, Margaret Wilson (Mrs. Henry Belin du Pont), 161, 210
Life of Eleuthère Irénée du Pont from Contemporary Correspondence (du Pont, Bessie G.), 119
Limerick house, *210*
Lindeberg, Harrie T., 22, 102–03, 106
Longwood Foundation, 79
Longwood house, 16–18, 23–24, 61, 72, *140*, *141*, 142, *143*, 160
Looms, Herter, 97

INDEX

Lord & Burnham greenhouses, 150
Lord, Ruth, 36
Louis XVI, King, 45
Louis XVI style, 85
Lower Louviers house, 17, 21, 23, 176, 203
Lunger, Harry W., 182–83, 186
Lunger, Mrs. Harry W. *See* du Pont, Jane
Lyndham house, 160, *205*

Maddox, George Amory, 202
Maddox, Mrs. George Amory. *See* du Pont, Alice
Mail-order houses, 167, 171
Martin, E. William, 22, 79, 173–74
Massachusetts Horticultural Society, 142
Massena & du Pont architects, 22, 88, 90, 167, 211
McConnell, James Hoge Tyler, 205
McCoy, Ann Brelsford (Mrs. George Weymouth), 24
McCoy, John W., 24
McIlhenney, Henry P., 186
McIntire, Francis, 202
McKim, Mead & White, 79
Meeds, Hollyday S., Jr., 204
Meeds, Mrs. Hollyday S., Jr. *See* du Pont, Ellen
Mellor, Meigs & Howe architects, 22, *30*, 34
Mellor, Walter, 34, 36–37. *See also* Mellor, Meigs & Howe
Meown Farm house, 23
Metropolitan Museum of Art American Wing (NY), 17, 132, 197
Modern conveniences, 16, 41, 78, 116, 121, 163, 177
Modern style, 150, 156, *157*, 187–91
Molas, Nicolas de, *29*, 37, *77*
Montgomery, Charles Berwind, 164
Montpelier plantation, 167
Moors lodge, The, 70
Moreton, Winnifred (Mrs. William Winder Laird, Jr.), 41–42
Morgan, Mrs. Richard. *See* du Pont, E. Frances
Morgan, Richard, 161, 163, 165
Mount Vernon (Virginia), 42, 210
Moxham, Catherine Dulcinea (Mrs. Eugene E. du Pont), 208
Mrs. Victor du Pont House, *207*
Mt. Cuba house, 13, *23*, 24, 141
Mullins, John, 211

National Highway Association, 70
National Register of Historic Places, 99, 205, 207
National Trust for Historic Preservation, 34
Neighborhood, The, 58, 62, 64
Nemours Foundation, 90, 202
Nemours house, 14–18, 21–22, 32, 141–42
Nemours, Pierre Samuel du Pont de, 14, 36, 41, 48, 55, 86
Neuville, Baroness Hyde de, *14*
Nevis mansion, 70
New York Times, The, 18, 142
Norman style, 183

Oberod, 182–86
Okie, R. Brognard, 22, 98, 160–61, 163–65, 186, 207, 209–11
Old Kennett Foundation, 174

Old Mill house, The, 70, *71*, *72*, *73*, 206
Old Nemours house, 23, 55, 68, 108, *181*
Ortiz, Julien de Villiers, 206
Osborne, Margaret (Mrs. William du Pont, Jr.), 169
Ostrander and Eshleman, 132, 134
Owl's Nest house, 18, 22–23, 161

Palladian design, 46, 106, 110
Parrish, Maxfield, 113
Peale, Rembrandt, 53, *54*, 113
Peirce's Park, 76–77
Pelleport, Gabrielle Josephine de la Fite de, 53
Pelleport house, 14–15, 51, 59, 205
Perot, Robeson Lea, 57, 64–65, 67, 110, 203, 205, 207
Peter Gregg Farm, 149
Phelps, Mary Kaye (Mrs. R. R. M. Carpenter Jr.), 211
Pierce-du Pont House, *75*, 76, 79–82
Point Lookout house, 205, 206
Port Royal country house, 135
Portraits, 14, *26*, 41, 53, *54*, 55, 78, 88, 110, 113, 188–89
Potter, William Woodburn, 65
Preservation Delaware, 99
Prohibition Era, 126
Public gardens, 76, 79, 99, 141, 169, 179
Pyle, Ethel (Mrs. Eugene du Pont Jr.), 102, 104
Pyle, Howard, 204

Queen Anne style, 25, 70, 72

Raley, Robert, 67
Reflections on the Wealth of a Nation (Nemours), 24
Regency style, 197
Renaissance style, 98, 132, 135
Rencourt house, 14–15, 59, *205*, 210
Ridgely, Ann (Mrs. Charles I. du Pont), 47
Ridgely house, 161, 211
Robinson, William, 134
Rokeby house, *203*
Roosevelt, Franklin Delano, Jr., 102
Ross, Donald, *75*, 79
Ross, Donald Peabody, 23, 148–50
Ross, Mrs. Donald Peabody. *See* du Pont, Wilhelmina
Rust, Gordon, 165

Sabatino, Di, 211
Saint Amour house, 15, 17, 21, 23, 76, 142, *145*, 146
Sargent, Charles Sprague, 142
Schleich Studios, 132
Schoemer, John R., 132, 134, 139
Schutt, Charles Porter, 208
Sears, Thomas, 23, *163*, 164–65, 177, 179, *180*, *185*, 186
Seybold, Joanne, 207
Sharp, Bayard, 98, 156
Sharp, H. Rodney, *22*, 92–93, 96–98, 119–20, 122, 156
Sharp, H. Rodney, Jr., 99
Sharp, Mrs. H. Rodney. *See* du Pont, Isabella
Shipman, Ellen, 23, 102, *104*, 106

— 225 —

Silliman, Henry Harper, 203
Simmons, Virginia (Mrs. S. Hallock du Pont), 209
Simons, Elise Wigfall (Mrs. Francis G. du Pont), 203
Singer, Frederick George Isaac, 122
Sleeper, Henry Davis, 132
Smith, Eleuthera du Pont, 14, 203
Smith, Thomas Mackie, 203
Smyth, James, 202–03
Spahr, Albert H., 113, 116, 208
Spanish style, 65
Spur, The, 86
Square House, The, 67
Squirrel Run house, 209
Stillpond house, *51*, 67–68, 142
Strand Millas house, 208, *209*
Swamp Hall, 15, 119, 203, *204*

T-Square Yearbook (AIA), 65
Teller, Myron, 164
Tenant houses, 63–64, 77, 79, 96, 132, 168, 179, 189, *192*, *193*, 208–09
Thomas Francis Bayard House, *206*
Thompson, Anne (Mrs. Ernest du Pont), 65
Thompson, James, 22, 149–50, 208
Town & Country, 86
Tudor style, 64, 72, 102–04
Tulip Hollow house, 23

University of Delaware, 24, 122, 204
University of Pennsylvania School of Architecture, 15
Upper Louviers, 46, *202*, 203
U.S. Rubber, 17
Utopian community, 51

Valley Garden Park, 74
Valmy house, *206*
Vaux, Baron Voruz de, *22*, 51, 78, 96–97
Victorian style, 17, 119
Villa d'Este (Italy), 36–37, 79
Vireaux house, 15, *204*
Vitale, Ferrucio, 211

Wagoner's Row house, 23, *211*
Wains, William, 67
Wales, John P., 204
Wallace & Warner architects, 124
Waterman, Thomas, 197, 200–201
Weir, Campbell, 160
Weir, Essie du Pont. *See* du Pont, Esther
Weir, Mrs. Campbell. *See* du Pont, Esther
Weller, Eleanor, 37
Westover Hills neighborhood (Wilmington, DE), 124
Weymouth, George A. "Frolic", 24
Weymouth, George Tyler, *10*, 208, 210
Weymouth, Mrs. George. *See* McCoy, Ann Brelsford
Wheelwright & Stevenson landscapers, 204
Wheelwright, Mrs. Robert. *See* du Pont, Ellen

Wheelwright, Robert, 74, 204
White Farmhouse, 160, 164
Who's Who of Commerce and Industry, 18
William Corbit house, 99
Wilmington & Northern Railroad, 14
Wilmington Stair, 23
Wilson, Paul E., 203
Windmar house, *64*, 68
Winterthur house, 15, 24, 46
    architects of, 23, 122
    furnishings of, 55, 197
    gardens of, 23, 141–42, *146*, *147*
    open to the public, 195, 197
    remodeling of, 21, 176
    vast size of, 18, 197
Winterthur Museum, 34, 200–201
Wood paneled rooms, 98, 113, 132, 163, 176–77
World War I, 16, 32, 39, 110
World War II, 79, 179, 197
Wrenn, Elizabeth (Mrs. S. Hallock du Pont), 160, 209
Wyeth, Ann, 24

Xanadu house (Cuba), 117

Yellin, Samuel, 65, 68, 97, 113, 208–09

ILLUSTRATION CREDITS

Andrew W. Edmonds Jr. - 123, 124, 125, 126, 127;
Archives of American Gardens - 105;
Art Institute of Chicago - 86, 91
Athenaeum of Philadelphia - 30
Brett Jones - 183, 184 (bottom), 185, 186
Carole Graham - 211
Carroll Morgan Carpenter - 158, 159, 160, 161, 162, 163, 164 Cornell University - 103, 104
Daphne Reese - 61
Delaware Historical Society - 49, 50
Dr. and Mrs. Ronald Finch - 209
Dr. and Mrs. William Norwood - 122
Everitt B. du Pont - 107, 109 (top), 110, 111
Franklin Delano Roosevelt Presidential Library - 102
Garden Club of America - 180 (bottom)
George A. Weymouth - 10
Hagley Museum & Library - 14, 15, 16, 20, 21, 22, 28, 29, 31, 32, 33, 34, 36, 37, 38, 39, 44, 45, 47, 48, 51, 52, 53, 58, 59, 60, 62, 63, 64, 67, 69, 70 (bottom), 71, 72, 73, 74, 79, 80, 81, 82 (top), 85, 92, 93, 94, 95, 96, 97, 101, 108, 112, 113, 114, 115, 117, 118, 121, 140, 141, 142, 143, 144, 145, 146, 147, 166, 167, 168, 182, 202, 203, 204, 208, 210
Henry B. du Pont - 210
Homsey Architects Inc. - 19, 40, 41, 42, 43, 151, 156, 157, 175, 176, 177, 178 (top), 179, 180 (top), 187, 188, 189, 190, 191, 192, 193, 211
Karen Farquhar - 71 (top), 203, 208
Lin and Henry White - 106
Longwood Gardens - 18, 75, 77, 78, 82 (bottom), 83

Lunger family - 185 (top)
Maggie Lidz - 76, 154, 207
Marion Lassen - 205
Mary Kaye Carpenter - 211
Michael Kahn - 24
Mr. and Mrs. Jamie Wyeth - 206
Mrs. William Gahagan - 66
Mt. Cuba Inc. - 181
Nancy Cooch - 205, 208
Nancy Greenewalt Frederick - 116, 170, 171, 172, 173, 174
Nemours Mansion & Gardens - 84, 87, 88, 89, 90, 202
Patt Cannon - 12
Pennsylvania State Archives - 165
Pierre and Martina Hayward - 210
Psychosynthesis Research Foundation - 206
Richard Dayton - 65, 109 (bottom), 128, 206
Richard S. du Pont - 209
Rick Darke - 25
Ross family - 68, 149, 150, 152, 153
Samuel Hobbs - 11
Sharp family - 98, 99, 155
Winterthur Archives - 17, 23, 26, 35, 46, 54, 55, 56, 57, 120, 129, 130, 131, 132, 133, 134, 135, 136, 137, 138, 139, 169, 195, 196, 197, 198, 199, 200, 201, 204, 205, 209, 210
Winterthur Library - 148, 178 (bottom), 194, 207
Winterthur Museum & Country Estate - frontispiece, 119
University of Delaware - 204, 207
University of Delaware Library - 100.